Lifelong Training
Triathlon

Advanced Training for Masters

Ironman Edition

Lifelong Training

TRIATHLON

Advanced Training for Masters

By Henry Ash, Barbara Warren

with a Foreword by Mark Allen

Published by Meyer & Meyer Sport

British Library Cataloguing in Publication Data
A catalogue record for this book is available from the British Library

Ash, Henry and Warren, Barbara:
Lifelong Training – Triathlon
Advanced Training for Masters
Oxford: Meyer & Meyer Sport (UK) Ltd., 2004
ISBN 1-84126-104-1

© 2004 by Meyer & Meyer Sport (UK) Ltd.
Aachen, Adelaide, Auckland, Budapest, Graz, Johannesburg,
Miami, Olten (CH), Oxford, Singapore, Toronto
Member of the World
Sports Publishers' Association (WSPA)
www.w-s-p-a.org
Printed and bound by: FINIDR, s. r. o.,Český Těšín
ISBN 1-84126-104-1
E-Mail: verlag@m-m-sports.com
www.m-m-sports.com

Contents

Foreword

By Mark Allen

We all have a Story

"Shortly before Kailua-Kona the first professionals came running toward me with long endurance strides. Mark Allen and Dave Scott were having their duel of the century. When I looked at them they gave the impression as if they had neither swum 2.4 miles nor cycled for 112 miles. Totally unbelievable! Later on I heard that they finished their marathon run in 2:40 and 2:41 hours. That's faster than my best time of 2:44 hours!"

Age-grouper Henry Ash's eyewitness account of what has become one of the greatest moments in triathlon history.

My human side wanted to have the perfect race, you know the one where you feel invincible every moment of the 140.6 miles an Ironman covers from start to finish. The movie projector inside my mind had played out a scenario where I led my greatest rival from the cannon blast and never had a chance to witness his race as he dropped further and further behind.

This had nothing to do with the reality on that day in 1989. I had bad patches where my legs screamed for me to quit. Scott was so strong I wasn't able to pull up even with him until mile seven of the marathon. The now famous decisive move came with less than two miles to go in the race, nearly 139 mile after the start cannon sounded. This was nothing like the parade of confidence and ease that I played out in my vision before the race.

This was the kind of race that unfolded in its own time, not on my schedule. It was seven years in the making, and took exactly 8:09:15 to mold into form. The rewards were many. But perhaps the greatest was an affirmation of life, of living powerfully and humbly, of overcoming the often noisy side that wants everything to go smoothly and uncovering the peaceful side that knows the greatest moments in life are rarely delivered by the hands of laziness and inactivity.

These are the riches of self-discovery that triathlons can provide, no matter who you are or what level you approach the sport with. All it takes is a modest amount of training and the will to throw yourself into the world of unpredictability that defines racing. In that realm you are the conduit that bonds together the duel worlds of control and surrender, of patience and speed, self-doubt and self-confidence, of knowing who you are and of discovering what that really means moment to moment.

The foundation for these experiences is built in training. Micro races happen each time you set foot out the door for a workout.

Every time you exercise you transform not only your body, but also enrich your heart and soul with the power of the air moving through you. Take away the distraction of figuring out how to train, and you become limitless in your ability to find peace through your workouts. Remove the guesswork of building your workout plan and you are free to tune into the body wisdom that can become your ultimate resource as a coach.

Do your runs with friends who make you laugh. Bike with a buddy and use the first few miles to spill your guts about what has been bothering you. Swim in a group and use camaraderie as motivation and inspiration for effort and consistency. These can become tools that are as essential in your journey through the sport as the information you have at your fingertips with this book.

We all have a story to tell. Mine has a happy ending, culminating six years after that first win with my sixth Ironman title. But the richness that I hold dear from all those years is universal. It is something called *Joy*. Not the ecstatic joy we often think about, but more the steady joy that comes from learning along the way. It comes by exploring. What is your top-end performance? Find out! What can you learn? The possibilities are limitless. Why read a book on triathlon training? Give it a glance through and be touched by the stories and experiences of others that lie inside. Then discover the story you have to tell as it unfolds before you.

This is life in the world of triathlon!

Mark Allen
Six-times Ironman Triathlon World Champion

Introduction

Nowadays sport is no longer a privilege for the younger generation, and definitely not endurance sport. The number of participants in today's triathlon events and in other forms of endurance sport such as cycling, cross-country skiing, to mention just a few, is a clear illustration of this. Often enough, it happens that those participants who have passed 40 (i.e. Masters) are even in the majority. Medical journals constantly point out that regular sport clearly enhances both life expectation and quality of life as one gets older. The ageing process of the heart, metabolism and muscular system is slowed down considerably. Cycling, continuous running and swimming are recommended as the most suitable here. Exactly the three forms of endurance sport are these that are united in triathlon. According to the doctors of sports medicine our bodies can be proved to be 'trainable' to the age of 80 and over. So it's never too late to begin with sport. There are numerous positive examples of this in triathlon.

It should be a person's aim to move on in age in good health. This is possible both through moderate physical exercise as well as with a competitive attitude, provided one pays attention to a few basic principles:

Training correspondent to your age implies:
▲ training with enjoyment, and not for all you're worth.
▲ training with a long term perspective and not a short one.
▲ training with a healthy ambitious attitude, not an over exaggerated one of grim determination.
▲ endurance training suitable for your age and not youthful sprint training.
▲ the certainty that you're not supplementing your inevitable day-to-day stress with sports stress.
▲ experiencing sport with your body, mind and soul, not only with your body.

Allow us to comment briefly on the term 'competition'. As regards Masters' participation in sports we are, in my opinion, not talking about a 'fight' or a 'contest', we have enough fights and contests in other areas of life as it is. At the very most it is a struggle with oneself, but never against others. It may be different in professional sport.

We have known for a long time now that we all must keep moving, it keeps us fit and healthy up to a great age. Thus, more exercise implies:

▲ Better health
▲ More *joie de vivre*
▲ Better well-being
▲ Better quality of life

This exercise does not begin with IRONMAN, but rather with banal tasks such as climbing stairs, walking, going shopping by bike, going to work on the bike or on foot instead of with the car.

An athlete whose training is oriented towards performance, wishes to see his own personal dream of success come true. Over the medium to long term this means more than just reeling off swimming, cycling and running miles. Body, spirit and soul together - the person as a whole - is what's needed.

To have managed it (finished) again, to feel better all round due to sport, to be able to show optimal condition and constitution, to be celebrated perhaps for one's performance, to stand on the winner's podium, to achieve one's best time, to have qualified - these can be the dreams of success in sport.

In order to achieve these targets, our bodies must be fit and healthy and we must adapt our performance to fit in with our own possibilities. This includes optimal 'tailor-made' training, a diet suitable to our needs, mental strength, well-adapted equipment and a general positive environment.

If it's difficult for even the professional triathletes to bring on their optimal performance at the right moment, it is even more difficult for those performance-oriented triathletes who have their career and family to consider as well.

Physical exertion is one side of the medal of our daily existence, the time factor is the other side. However let us be comforted by the fact that statisticians have discovered that adults in 1999 spent a large amount of time daily in front of the TV, e.g. in France and Germany 198 minutes, in Italy 229 minutes, in England 232 minutes and in the USA 259 minutes. This is on average 3-4 hours daily. So accordingly, there must also be time for some sensible, enjoyable endurance training. And anyone who makes use of only 1-2 hours for his triathlon training in the middle of the year will, with the right training, undoubtedly be able to successfully compete in the Middle and Ironman distances.

Therefore according to statistics, an athlete who trains 1-2 hours daily in the middle of the year will still be able to watch TV for more than 2 hours. When looked at this way, the time factor cannot really be seen as a major handicap.

Masters - an Example to Young Men and Women

At this stage we would like to refer to some of the many Master triathletes who have turned into idols for a large number of young athletes. This didn't necessarily have to do with their finishing times in competition, but rather with the way they have taken on challenges and the mental attitude they mastered these challenges with.

Here are a few examples:

▲ The 'Twin Team', Dr. BARBARA WARREN and her twin sister ANGELIKA; who keep on giving amazing performances even in their late 40s. Be it the many several Ironman events in Hawaii, the De Sables marathon, runs of over 95 miles from Death Valley up to the highest peak - the 4 300m high Mount Withney - or the successful participation in the RAAM (Race Across America) - the 3 400 miles long run across the USA.

▲ Dave SCOTT, six times Winner of the Ironman Hawaii, who in his mid-forties was still up among the top five in the Ironman Hawaii.

▲ The 73 year old Hans PLAJER who caused great rejoice and euphoria when finishing the Austrian Ironman after a good 16 hours.

▲ The 64 year old Ludwig AMARELL, who as well as crossing Finland a number of times on skis, completed his first Ironman competition with a time of 12:08 hours.

▲ Kalli NOTTRODT, who can be proud of his extremely successful record of success in his first decade as a Master.

There are more Master athletes of this caliber in every region, in many cities and clubs all around the world.

With this book we would like to continue on from the book "Lifelong Success - Triathlon: Training for Masters." This deals with the fundamental considerations for Master sports, as well as the complete training program for newcomers and experienced athletes over the Novice and Short Distances.

All the problems associated with the longer triathlon distances i.e. the Middle and Ironman Distances are explained in detail in this second volume of the Master series. We're not just talking about facts, numbers, heart rates, training miles etc but also about increasing motivation. Without sufficient suitable motivating force for systematic triathlon training, even a keen and ambitious athlete will not derive enjoyment from his sport for long.

Most triathletes dream of successful participation in an Ironman, and thus find themselves on an enticing path which requires three steps.

Dream, vision, the first step. The mental basis is laid here.
Goal, the second step. This is about planning realistic goals for keeping the entire path intact.
Ironman, the third step. What we mean here is carrying it out, implementing the planned training, and the finish.

It is on this path (dream - goal - Ironman) with its three big steps and numerous little inches, that we would like to accompany you, so that you can fulfill your dream of an Ironman finish.

Seeing the Entire Aspect of Sports Activity

Athletic performance, or the acknowledgment that it receives, should never depend just on the finishing time in a competition, but rather we Masters should look at all the aspects of our sports activity.

A sense of contentment and harmony with one's own body is a basic requirement for an athlete's self-confidence and self-esteem, regardless of his age, career, social standing, descent or advanced abilities.

It is particularly important for athletes who have problems with their self-esteem to experience a feeling of success through their personal fitness or performance capacity. In all our observations we always take in an athlete in his entirety, seeing the complete athlete, the complete person.

What we mean here is the athlete who does not only train with his body, but rather makes use of his mind and lets his psyche, his soul take effect. The motto here is "heart, hand and mind," i.e. the triathlete who goes about his sport with the right physical, psychic and mental attitude. We Masters can and should draw on that extra bit of life experience that we have, compared to the younger athletes, and then set an example.

There is no doubt that scientific discoveries are of great importance here. However, we don't wish to be constantly referring to statistical data and scientific facts as there are plenty of examples which cannot be explained scientifically e.g. from a scientific point of view a bumble bee weighing 1.2 grams with a wing circumference of only 0.7 cm^2 will never be able to fly - but yet it can!

Apart from all our physical effort and common sense, we Masters should not forget to let our feelings, our emotions take effect. People without much feeling are still to be pitied. In order to show just how vital this is, Chapter 11 gives a detailed description of an athlete's feelings and emotions during an Ironman spectacle in Hawaii.

So with this in mind, we wish us all many enjoyable hours of training and successful competitions!

Your team of authors

Henry and Barbara

CHAPTER 1

Performance-Oriented Training

A Master who carries out his sport with ambition, i.e. aimed towards performance, possesses a special portion of motivation for his sport. Such athletes ask themselves:

▲ How good is my performance?
▲ Where are my limits in sport?
▲ How can I train optimally, so as to improve my times, to get through the qualification, to be first in my age group, to reach my performance limit?

This training is then set towards a certain performance target. Achieving good performances or getting to know one's own personal limits is a fascinating matter. Most Master sportsmen are not professional athletes and have already surpassed their absolute zenith of performance. For this reason, when looking at performance, we must always take our personal circumstances - our situation - into consideration.

As triathlon is carried out at both competitive and hobby levels, I would like to illustrate the following sub-categories based on experience:

	Hours of training per year	Hours of training per week
Training as a hobby	up to 365	up to 7
Performance Training Systematic Training (ambitious athletes)	up to 730	7 - 14 hours
Top Performance Training- athletes who are particularly motivated by performance	more than 730	> 14 hours

Every ambitious triathlete is going to ask himself, "How can I continue to improve my performance?" The most important factor here is one's health.

The Medical Examination

When looking at performance at all levels, top priority should be maintaining one's health. An optimal performance in triathlon must be subordinate in ranking to one's health. After all, the aim is to minimize health risks at the same time. Thus we can assign an optimal sports performance between the best possible state of health and the minimum amount of risks.

| Best possible state of health | **Optimal sports performance** | Minimum amount of risks |

In order to aim for the minimum amount of risks through physical activity, every keen athlete in training should go for a general medical examination once a year. Needless to say more frequent check-ups are necessary when health problems arise. This is particularly the case for Masters who are taking on new challenges e.g the first ever participation in a Middle or Ironman distance.

A successful medical examination is the ticket to individual custom-made training.

Masters should go to a doctor for a routine check-up once a year in the preparation period, when extensive training starts.

The check-up includes:
▲ Heart diagnosis
▲ ECG at rest and under exercise
▲ Lung Diagnosis
▲ Diagnosis of blood and urine
▲ CRP rate (C-reactive protein).

Participation in endurance sports - which is what we have in triathlon - has, for Masters in particular, a preventative effect regarding cardiovascular illnesses and this is a fact that has been confirmed in many examinations. What is specifically implied here is high blood pressure, heart attack, stroke and arteriosclerosis. The factor in our blood centre responsible for this **CRP** (C -reactive acute phase protein) attaches itself to pathogenes (disease-causing agents). This blood rate is reduced dramatically by physical activity. A high CRP rate needs to be treated as it clearly indicates a hardening of the arteries. Prof. UHLENBRUCK concluded from this that 2 000 to 2 500 kcal per week are to be burned up through sport, in order to be able to perceive notice-able possible effects on one's health. Thus his recommendation of making CRP a fixed component of a general fitness check. Provided of course that one does not have a cold or an infection, as this temporarily leads to high rates.

The examination focuses on the cardiovascular system, which is at times subject to enormous strain and exertion. Illness or damage of whatever kind can unexpectedly lead to heart problems and even to sudden cardiac death. We are all familiar with the

startling reports on this theme. Examinations carried out under maximal load show that there is a 56% risk of sudden cardiac death for a person with a bad training state as opposed to 5% for someone with a better training state.

At a young age it is normally caused by congenital heart disease, damage to the heart muscle including damage caused by infection.

As one gets older cardiac incidents are more often due to coronary disease. According to PROCHNOW, it is those older athletes who subject themselves to high and intensive training loads who are **most likely to be at risk here**. The same is true for those who take up training again after a long pause as well as people with risk factors and accompanying illnesses.

Luckily enough there is no need for us to get panicky, as before something happens, there are several protective mechanisms in our body which get to work.

▲ Dizziness and temporary unconsciousness
▲ Inexplicable drops in performance
▲ Shortness of breath
▲ Cardiac arrythmia and cardialgia
▲ Infection
▲ General weakness
▲ Fever

Should these problems arise, training is totally taboo and one must consult a doctor.

An athlete who ignores these warning signals, and sticks to his training plans regardless of the consequences, needn't wonder if more serious damage has been caused.

It is not physical activity that is the cause here but rather illness, which has either not been recognized or has been ignored due to some pathological ambition.

CHAPTER 2

Training for the Middle and Long Distances

Before an athlete starts off training for the middle and long distances he should ask himself the following self-critical question:

"What requirements must I fulfill in order to build in these distances, or better the mastering of these distances into my sports target planning?"

Closely related to this is the question regarding one's objective.

We have to make a clear difference here: is it the Middle distance that I'm interested in or do I intend to take up the greatest challenge of all, the Ironman Distance? They are targets worth aiming for, when we have the correct attitude and are able to include our own personal situation into our realistic perspective. Everyone can build castles in the air and dream of victory in a Middle triathlon; we are not forbidden to dream of victory in an Ironman triathlon, or even at the Hawaii Ironman, but for most of us it's far too far away. In short: unrealistic. Let's deal with realistic circumstances instead and keep both feet on the ground.

Yeah I know, but to win would be great! But is winning so important in our sporting activity?

I have already given a detailed opinion on this matter.

However, each one of us can be successful when our judgment is realistic. And we reach this success when we reach our target, when we have mastered the challenge we had set for ourselves, when we have managed to get through it all, when we have **finished**! Everyone can achieve this success when they go about their task realistically. With 500 starters, only one person can be the overall winner, i.e. in numerical terms, the chance of being the overall winner is 0.2%. In the case of 1,800 starters - which is common in Ironman competitions - the chance of victory is exactly 0.055%.

So, let's try to stay realistic and prepare ourselves for our own success.

What Requirements Should I Fulfill for the Middle Distance?

I deliberately do not say 'must I fulfill', as opinions and viewpoints vary here. The athlete who just desperately wants to complete the Middle Distance, only to be able to tell his grandchildren about his heroic deed, is not exactly the athlete I wish to look at. What I'm talking about is a solid framework for the Middle distance and later for the Ironman Distance. One should not complete these distances for all one's worth, but with great enjoyment and with a satisfying feeling of success. These are the only conditions for deriving long term enjoyment from this sport and being able to profit sufficiently from the numerous benefits (see Lifelong Success - Triathlon: Training for Masters, Chapters 3 and 4).

In Chapter 1 I have already explained the health-related requirements in detail. It's in a triathlete's blood to look for new challenges and take them on. For athletes who have successfully completed the Short distance of 1 500m swimming, 40km cycling and 10km running, and want to make the "IRONMAN" dream come true, the Middle distance is a giant step in this direction.

The distances in the Middle triathlon are:
1.2 miles swimming
56 miles cycling
13 miles running

This is also referred to as the '**half-distance**'. There is a simple explanation for this. The Ironman, being the measure of all things in triathlon, is referred to as the '*Single Distance*'. Half of that is thus the **Half- or Middle Distance**, a quarter of it the **Quarter Distance**. The latter term would approximately apply to the short/ Olympic distance.

In the Middle triathlon we are dealing with three complete endurance disciplines in themselves, all of which demand regular training. These distances are unsuitable for newcomers as each of these three endurance sports requires a certain standard of training if one wants to avoid any health risks. Athletes who cross over from other forms of endurance sport are of course more likely to manage this transition, as they already have a good basic level of fitness in the first place. This is most likely the case for marathon runners and good touring cyclists, due to their well-built muscles and high agility. These athletes can often make up for any swimming problems they may have with strong cycling and running performances.

On this Middle distance you will find either triathletes who, in the medium to long term, want to get to grips with the Ironman distance or the Ironman athletes themselves. The latter like to use this distance as a 'dress rehearsal' four weeks before an Ironman competition.

Good conditions for successfully completing the Middle distances:

1. **Two years of regular endurance training.**
2. Participation in a half-marathon.
3. Cycling tours covering 50-60 miles.
4. Swimming sessions covering 2,000 to 3,000yds.
5. Two years experience with the novice and short distances.

It is very difficult to say exactly how many competitions an athlete should take part in during a season, as the middle distance is often completed in alternation with Ironman distances.

As a rough guide for triathletes who only take part in short and middle triathlons, I would say:

Master Newcomers: 2-4 short distances plus 2 middle distances.

More Ambitious Masters: 2-6 short distances and 2-3 middle distances.

What Requirements Should I Fulfill for the Ironman Distance?

The magical Ironman Distance is composed of the following:
2.4 miles swimming
112 miles cycling
26 miles running,
in total therefore a distance of 140 miles.

At the back of every triathlete's mind is the notion: ".Just to have a go at the Ironman distance one day, and then.....?" So, and then, you set yourself the dream of the real Hawaii Ironman as a target and can make it come true. However this tremendous sporting hurdle can only be overcome by Masters with very good endurance training.

Anyone who has managed several short and middle distances and is willing to have a go at the Ironman distance, has the right requirement for being successful in this distance too. But putting it into practice is not easy in all matters. Apart from physical training, mental attitude is of utmost importance.

On the other hand, an athlete who thinks that he mentally has difficulties with this 'Ironman' mammoth, he is very much mistaken. Everyone who wants to have a go at this distance has these initial mental difficulties and problems.

Nobody manages this distance without preparation. Luckily enough this sporting adventure is not available for sale in the stores. Each individual athlete must achieve this goal by himself, through sensible, balanced and calm endurance training.

Good conditions for successfully completing Ironman Distances are:

1. Systematic triathlon training over a number of years.
2. Successful completion of several Middle distances.
3. Participation in marathon runs.
4. Cycling tours of 95 miles.
5. Swimming sessions of 3 000 to 4 000yds.

Target Competition Times

An athlete wishing to complete the Middle or Ironman distance for the first time is bound to think a lot about his possible finishing times. Results on the Short or Middle distance can be helpful as well as competition times by a triathlete at more or less the same level. Be careful with such comparisons though. Triathlete X is just as fast as myself on the Short distance, so therefore I will have exactly the same times as he does on the Ironman Distance. A good 'sprinter' for the Short distance is by no means a good 'stayer' over the long distances.

Many Masters can achieve a finishing time of 12 or 13 hours for the magical 140 miles in their very first Ironman competition.

The requirements for this are systematic training and the appropriate general situation. To hit the 10 hour mark as an advanced Master is something which demands extraordinary conditions. Included here are a considerably higher training effort, good competitive opportunities, an extra portion of stamina, willpower, talent in endurance and an all-round positive situation. A 'push-up' in training, which is how several young athletes manage to do it, does not make much sense for Masters, as it often leads to health problems and then to a much too rapid end of sporting ambitions.

Triathlon, the combination of three endurance sports, requires continuous training over a number of years. For this reason it is only possible to plan success in triathlon in the medium to long term, and only those athletes who have enough patience to to train systematically over a number of years can be sure to achieve this success. Let me clarify this by comparing this process to a marathon runner. Every experienced marathon runner knows that the actual marathon itself only begins around the 20 mile mark. Anything up to this does not count any more. From mile 20 onwards the real work begins. An athlete who shoots his bolt on the first 6, 12 or 18 miles, pays dearly for this past the 18 mile mark. The secret is to wait patiently up to mile 18. In the case of the Ironman this patience is put under much longer and much more intensive strain than for a marathon run. This is not only true in competition but also particularly in the build-up of training over many years.

For this reason, before taking part in his first Ironman, an athlete's aim should simply be to **finish**. In order to take account of the great number of Master participants present, competition times have been extended to 17 hours in all Ironman competitions.

Partner-friendly Training

Success or lack of success in triathlon for every Master athlete, who still goes out to work, depends on how he manages to integrate his intensive training into his daily routine, and particularly to what extent he can manage it timewise. Masters who have already retired from work on the other hand have an advantage here, which enables them to carry out their training more calmly and systematically.

Long routes to get to training worsen the conditions considerably for working Masters in particular. To prevent this, every athlete should take a good look at his overall situation and envi-

ronment to see if he can make effective use of one or more of the following possibilities for training:

- ▲ Cycling to work on the bike every day. Certain detours enable you to carry out training as desired.
- ▲ Spend time in an indoor pool before going to work.
- ▲ Go for a swim or a run at lunchtime.
- ▲ Run to work on several days.
- ▲ When visiting friends or relatives let the family take the car and you go by bike.
- ▲ Head off to work either with public transport or with a colleague, and run the way home.
- ▲ Have one or more members of your family accompany you on your run with their bike.
- ▲ When on holidays, do cycling training in the mornings from 7-9 o'clock; there's not much traffic then, the temperature is pleasant and you have the rest of the day free to do what you'd like.
- ▲ When swimming in a lake, have your family accompany you in a boat.
- ▲ Visit outdoor swimming pools together with the family.

As you can see there are several ways to set out your training, in such a way that the strain on your family is cut down.

As well as organizing training cleverly like this, I also find it very important to include the family, girlfriend/boyfriend in your sporting activities. If your partner or family don't just sullenly accept, but rather actively support you with your sport, this is very beneficial to your sporting development. In return we should spend long weekends, short breaks and beautiful holidays together with our partners, where triathlon is not the only point on the agenda.

With a little imagination it is possible to extend this partner-friendly triathlon even further.

CHAPTER 3

Planning the Triathlon Year

Any keen or ambitious master competing in triathlon ought to organize his training in such a way that he can attain the best performance capacity possible given the amount of time he has at his disposal. In principle it doesn't matter at all if you spend five, seven, ten or even fifteen or more hours training per week. A triathlon year, in order to be as successful as possible, is divided up into separate time periods, taking account of three important training principles at all times.

These three most important training principles are:

1. Increasing training loads

Triathlon training which is monotonous in intensity and volume will not lead to any significant improvements in an athlete's performance. Athletes who divide their year up into time periods differing in training volume and intensity will experience considerable improvements. Numerous systems of function in our body react to exertion by adapting appropriately. This is one of our body's protective mechanisms, so as not to be brought to its absolute performance limit again under similar exertion.

2. From general to specific load

The first task at the beginning of the triathlon season is to prepare the athlete's systems of function (such as his cardio-vascular system and general athletic abilities) for the oncoming exertive loads. This does not necessarily have to occur through swimming, cycling or running, but also by using cross-country skiing, speed skating or a fitness studio. As regards strength endurance, this would imply training general endurance and strength separately at first, and then moving on to specific strength endurance in the next preparation stages.

3. Load and recovery in alternation

One often underestimates the fact that the actual growth in performance that we aim for in training does not occur during the load phase, but rather is achieved only in the recovery period. This circumstance is referred to as **super compensation**. This implies that an improvement in performance does not occur during an exertive 90 mile-long cycling session, but in the recovery phase to follow. An athlete who does not grant his body enough time for recovery, will experience a drop in performance instead of a rise. We Masters have to allow our bodies more time for recovery than a 20-30 year old athlete does. The interesting thing is that after a sufficient recovery phase our performance capacity exceeds the level we started off with. So we just have to grant our body this break, if we want to see improvements in performance. This holds for during the week, within the month and in particular throughout the year.

Just as with the Short distances, a systematic structure for a year's training for the long triathlon distances consists of three time periods of different duration:

▲ Preparation period (I and II)
▲ Competition period
▲ Transitional period

The individual time periods obviously depend on the competition dates among other things. For athletes whose competitions are from June to September or October, one can recommend the following:

Preparation period:	February-May	four months
Competition period:	June-September	four months
Transitional period:	October-January	four months

The following can be recommended for younger or ambitious Masters:

Preparation period:	February-May	four months
Competition period:	June to October	five months
Transitional period:	November-January	three months

Preparation Period

Creating basic endurance is the main priority in the first section of the preparation period. The foundation is laid for the more intensive training of the second section and the competition period. Volume is systematically increased at low to medium load intensity. Nevertheless one must still pay attention to recovery and regeneration as already mentioned. One trains mainly according to the **continuous method**. Due to the weather conditions it is mostly running and swimming training that takes place. Cross-country skiing or cycling on the 'roller' also improves basic endurance. Strength endurance training can also enhance one's overall condition in these months.

Because of varying weather conditions it can be wise to divide up winter and spring training into so-called **blocks**. This block training can be as follows: January - swimming month, February - running month, March - cycling month. It is also possible to defer everything for a month, or to swop the running and swimming month. More details of this can be found in the training recommendations.

Combination training, in particular the cycle-run change, is added onto the agenda from April onwards. This is in order to be better able to cope with the transitions in competition.

Possible Variations for Combination Training cycle-run:

▲ Short, brisk cycling session + long, relaxed run
▲ Long, relaxed cycling session + short, brisk run
▲ Short, brisk cycling session + short, brisk run

Important for the entire preparation period is the adjustment between weeks of normal load and regenerative load (see Chapters 9 and 10).

Once a week throughout the entire preparation period one must have carried out a very long training session of low intensity. This does not necessarily apply to newcomers; a long run or a cycle over a number of hours is what can be recommended for them. These sessions are for fat-burning, a particularly important element for endurance sportsmen.

The Competition Period

Now it's getting exciting. The competition period goes on for 4-5 months for the ambitious triathletes. It begins at the end of May or beginning of June and stretches into September; for those with Hawaii as their target, as far as October. No triathlete can be in top form throughout this entire period. Nevertheless it is advisable to set oneself two to a maximum of three triathlon highlights.

The first section of this phase is taken up with 'build-up' competitions. These give the athlete the opportunity to test out not only form and materials, but also various tactics and eating habits. Sometimes intensive training still takes place between these first test triathlons, except for the last three days. Normal training sessions alternate with relaxed ones, normal weeks with easy or regenerative weeks. One must make sure to have sufficient regeneration after each competition. This obviously depends on the triathlon distance, one's state of training and one's age. Athletes with a very good state of training regenerate more quickly than others. Younger Master athletes similarly regenerate faster than older Masters. The intensity of the competition also plays a decisive role. If this lies at about 90%, instead of the usual 100%, recovery time will also be considerably shorter.

Two to three weeks are required for regeneration after a Middle triathlon; after an Ironman competition three to even four. Needless to say one should not take part in any further competitions at this time. After this time normal training begins again. Although I am familiar with all the facts here I must confess that I too have 'sinned' in this matter.

The number of competions an athlete enters in a year depends first and foremost on the distance itself, but also on the athlete's training state, age and attitude. With attitude I mean the following: there are several triathletes who complete competitions quite easily and you can really see the fun they have doing triathlon.

This also includes the enjoyment they have comparing themselves with others in a fair contest and not fighting against them. Other athletes, however, do it all with grim determination, believe that triathlon is the most important thing in the world and put themselves under enormous mental strain in the process. They have not recognised at all that our sport should also be fun.

When an athlete has found his form in the course of the season and confirmed this in a competition, he will to a large extent do relaxed training between further oncoming triathlon competitions. Training volume is reduced.

The Transition Period (Major Regeneration)

Unfortunately many Masters underestimate the real purpose of the transition period and of major regeneration. This phase is of utmost importance both for a triathlete's long-term performance development as well as for his health.

The genuinely calm months of the year begin for a triathlete immediately after the last competition of the season. As this triathlon is also nearly always the last seasonal highlight, his batteries are low anyway. Every triathlete looks forward to the oncoming easy months of relaxed training. In this transitional period, nobody should suddenly come up with the bright idea of quickly adding on the new cross-country running season. Such an undertaking might work well for a year or two. At some stage or other our body will get its well-earned rest in the form of injuries, often long-term injuries.

At the end of a season, which has really sapped his strength, a triathlete simply needs major regeneration, especially the ambitious Master. At last he has the time and leisure on his hands to look after those hobbies which for time reasons have been neglected throughout the year. At the top of this hobby list should

be his relationships with other people, i.e. more intensive contact with friends, acquaintances and of course one's own family. In short, the triathlete is supposed to recover both physically and mentally during this period, and gather new strength and motivation for the next season in the process. The motivation factor is frequently underestimated. An athlete who is not motivated is not able to bring out performance. Motivation is one of the prerequirements for successful participation in triathlon. It represents the willingness for sytematic training.

Training is easy-going and minimal in volume. Several pounds of winter fat are the (correct!) visible evidence of good regeneration. Obviously one must also cut down on the extensive diet from the preparation period as there is now a large drop in daily energy demand. One should also be sure to take a critical look-back at the entire season. Questions like: Was my preparation correct? Did I set my seasonal highlights right? Did my results match my possibilities? Was training all right in volume and intensity? Did I successfully manage to separate career, private life and sport? Questions upon questions, all of which are to be answered self-critically.

Not to forget of course the outstanding question: were effort and benefit in the right proportion for me personally?

So as not to forget these hopefully honest answers, it's a good idea to write all this into our training diary.

It is not possible to answer these questions when we have not kept daily record of our training.

A further possibility for major regeneration after several intensive years is to put in a so-called **active year of rest**. Many choose the last year in a particular age category for this, so as not only to dream about the Hawaii Ironman in the next age group, but also to make this dream come true. An athlete who really actively recovers in this year by continuing to train at low volume and mainly in the area of basic endurance can particularly look forward to his first year in his new age group.

More details on how to sensibly organize training in this phase can be found in the appropriate training chapters.

CHAPTER 4

Running

The most Difficult Discipline?

General Errors in Running Training

Before I look at correct running training in more detail, I would like to point out typical running errors so as to save you from having to confront them in the first place:

Wrong attitude

An athlete who goes about his sporting goals with grim determination will not be doing triathlon sport for long. Fun is one of the most important motives for our fascinating sport. Never stick to rigid training plans. You'd do better to cancel a training session than to be under permanent pressure. Just as important is satisfaction with our performances in competition. After investing a lot of time and quite often a good bit of money for training, why should we be so dissatisfied with our achievements? Our triathlon sport ought to be compensation for our day to day stress factors among other things. Why should we have even more stress due to results which we didn't manage to achieve?

Wrong diet

Every car driver knows that he has to fill his tank with suitable fuel of high technical quality. Similarly an athlete who demands a lot from his body must also provide it with correct food and drink. Anyone who sees his body as an incinerator, is not going to bring medium to long-term performance.

Lack of planning

Anyone wishing to improve his performance requires realistic targets to aim for. Training planning starts out at the current performance level. Keeping a training diary helps you to identify any errors and correct them as early as possible.

Too high a tempo

Masters who keep on training at a tempo that is too high, are constantly reaching their performance limits. They are only weakening themselves and are not able to increase their performance in competition.

Too much training

Performance suffers under too much as well as too little training. Therefore every Master must find out for himself what amount of training and what intensity is right for him.

Too many competitions

Anyone who feels he has to compete in one or even two triathlon competitions every weekend - cross-country runs in winter, numerous marathon runs in spring and autumn - shouldn't be surprised about the onset of injuries, illnesses, lack of motivation, monotony, social isolation and other negative aspects. He encourages all these negative 'side effects' and his quality of life suffers considerably in the process.

Going without sufficient regeneration

A recovery phase must take place after all sporting activity, otherwise our body will burn out and our performance capacity will drop instead of improving. Even the most ambitious Master must allow himself one or two days without sport. An athlete not wishing to overdo his performance abilities can have two or three 'sport-free' days in the week. Particularly important is major regeneration in autumn and winter; this should last for several months.

Problems with motivation

Setting new targets for oneself, participation in special competitions, training within a group, varying training intensity and volume as well as days involving no sport can improve and renew motivation.

No stretching

Our muscles become more supple and and develop better functional abilities with appropriate stretching exercises. It is common knowledge that only one of every three runners stretches regularly and sufficiently. Stretching exercises enhance the muscles' elasticity and improve the flexibility of the joints thus preventing overstrain.

A Few Hints For Running

A total of 42 tips for the half-marathon and marathon runs should help you train for this triathlon discipline - generally considered to be the most difficult of all three - in such a way that the frequent apprehension beforehand changes to one of anticipation.

14 Tips For Running Training

▲ You need to do six long runs (16 - 20 miles) in marathon preparation, without long cycling sessions.

▲ Four long runs (16, 17, 18, 19 miles) are needed in marathon preparation when you have also completed 3-4 long cycling sessions (> 60 miles).

▲ In the last three months before a marathon, run the marathon distance at least per week, i.e.at least 26 miles.

▲ In the last two training weeks reduce training drastically. Go to the start with a guilty conscience about the last 10 days of training.

▲ Vary your training routes. Go on a 'running visit' to friends, this is motivating and saves a lot of time.

▲ Having training partners motivates you to train regularly. However, it must be a partner whose running tempo matches well with your own. The weaker runner sets the running pace. It should never turn into group pressure where the strongest athlete sets the pace.

▲ Humerous conversation during training brings a smile to your face!

▲ When running, breathe down to your stomach, this type of breathing is more effective than chest breathing. With chest breathing only the top of the lung is used, whereas the entire lung is used when breathing with the stomach. You can practice this using this book. Lie on your back, and place this book on your stomach. As you breathe in and out, the book slowly rises and falls.

▲ Running in hilly areas strengthens the leg muscles.

▲ Make your training partner-friendly. If your partner doesn't run with you, he/she can perhaps accompany you on a bike. Incorporate fitness into your leisure activities together.

▲ Complete training both with and without a pulse measurer. That way we protect ourselves from becoming 'slaves' to these devices.

▲ Days without any training are part of a triathlete's routine. Without appropriate regeneration we cannot achieve and retain a good level of performance.

▲ There are more important things in life than swimming, cycling and running. Included here are family, career, friends, partners. A triathlete is not a 'swimruncyclist', but rather a person who also happens to be a sportsman.

▲ Do not train monotonously, but rather with variety. This not only raises motivation, but also our performance capacity in endurance sport. This is *the* secret to success for ambitous Masters.

14 Tips for a proper diet

▲ Strengthen your immune system. Triathletes are more vulnerable to infection during the intensive training phase than they are doing normal training. This is true for training camps in particular. After a long training session our white blood corpuscles are less capable of combatting any invading viruses. For this reason we are more prone to catching colds. On long training sessions we should take a sports drink with us which has a 25% glucose content among other nutrients. This activates our white blood corpuscles. Half a gram of Vitamin C per day reduces the risk of catching colds. With the first signs of a cold, it's wise to do no training or simply only regenerative training.

▲ Avoid stress and get sufficient sleep. When training volumes are high, one should try and avoid stress where at all possible.

However, who is always able to do this in our career or in our family? Sufficient sleep protects our immune system and one simply needs more sleep as training increases. There is a simple formula for this when running: for every additional 12 miles a week, our body requires a half hour more sleep every night.

▲ Eat and drink more with higher training loads. In the first few hours following training our body stores nearly all carbohydrates. We should make use of this for the intake of additional energy during the intensive training phase. Sufficient and regular drinking before and after training is not only necessary in summer but in winter too. Drink a glass of water every hour, particularly drink a lot with meals and after training. Be careful with tea, coffee and alcohol as they dehydrate our body.

▲ Practice drinking on runs that go on for more than two hours. A mixture of apple juice and still mineral water (1:1:1) contains the necessary amount of carbohydrates (approx. 50g/l), still water the necessary amounts of sodium, potassium, calcium and magnesium.

▲ Particularly in the last days coming up to a marathon eat a lot of proteins. Proteins stimulate our brain function whereas animal fats slow this down.
Brain foods are: seawater fish, sardines, herring, tuna, beetroot, carrots, celery, barley, wholewheat rice, oats, lean beef, dried bean sprouts, nuts and seeds, dark-green and orange fruit and vegetables, grapes, pears, apples, basil, ginger, liquorice, rosmarine, wheatgerm, brewer's yeast and lecithin.

▲ Be sparing with fat.
▲ On the evening before the marathon eat your last high-carbohydrate meal at lunchtime. Eat fish in the evening. Drink a lot during the day.

▲ Have a light breakfast 2-3 hours before the marathon. Two slices of white bread with honey, sugar-beet syrup and jam. Maybe a banana as well. Coffee has a diuretic effect and should be avoided.

▲ Organize your drink supplies for the run in plenty of time.

▲ Drink regularly up to about half an hour before the run starts.

▲ Begin drinking early enough during competition - in warm weather from 5km onwards and otherwise after 10km; drink a full beaker every 15 minutes.

▲ Find out beforehand what drinks are handed out during the marathon. If not familiar with certain drinks, you should definitely dilute them half and half first.

▲ Solid food is not necessary, perhaps some little pieces of banana or sponge cake.

▲ After the marathon: the same obviously holds for after a triathlon - begin with fluid and carbohydrate intake as soon as possible. Bread, raisins, pasta, rice, potatoes, cake, soup, and diluted fruit juice are particularly suitable here.

14 Tips for Competition

▲ Set realistic targets and interim targets.

▲ Be sure to take account of weather conditions and type of route when planning.

▲ Only use shoes and socks that are already 'worn in'.

▲ Put Band-Aids over nipples to prevent chafing.

▲ If you didn't sleep much during the last night, you needn't worry. More important is the night before. Your body is rested anyway due to the drastic reduction in training in the last week.

▲ Before the start make sure that your shoes fit comfortably and that you've made a double knot. In hot temperatures be sure to wear a cap.

▲ Run half-marathons and marathons at the steadiest pace possible. The steadier the run, the lesser the drop in performance on the last section of the run.

▲ Keep to the correct running tempo on the first few miles in particular. You can check your times for the first miles with your stop and heart rate monitor. The correct exertion heart rate sets in during mile 2 and this should stay more or less constant up to about mile 21. Then it rises.

▲ Divide up the 26 miles into 3-mile stages. While running occupy yourself wtih the following thoughts:

3-mile mark, only warmed up now; 6-mile mark is an important through station, I might have to change my target time here already. 9-mile mark, have already managed more than a third. 12 miles, nearly halfway there. Was the second 6 mile stage ok? Half-marathon, first half is behind me! On comes the second half! 15 miles, an important cornerstone. Slowly but surely the marathon is beginning now. Only another 11 miles! 18-mile mark, the third sixer, only another 8 miles to go. From here on I'm counting the miles backwards. Only 7,6,5 no more looking at my pulse, 4,3, it's not normally worth putting on my running shoes for only 3 miles - and here I am already at the 23 mile mark. It's getting difficult, it's allowed to be difficult, now's the proof whether I've trained properly. It's getting exciting. By keeping up a steady pace one overtakes many competitors. So, only another 2 miles, my projection of a realistic finishing time is running at full steam. A feeling of anticipation, just one more mile, one mile only. The last mile is the best mile of the whole run, this is what I trained for, I have success at my feet. There are so many people who are only here because of me, I can't let them down now, the loud speakers, I feel I've got wings, only a few more yards, the finishing flag, I did it, I finished! I'm the winner, yes, I'm my very own winner!

▲ In the case of cramp, stretch the muscles until it subsides.

▲ If you get a stitch in your side, breathe out slowly and deeply, run on calmly.

▲ If it gets tough; try and distract yourself from your difficulties by
  * taking in the scenery around you
  * guessing your kilometer times
  * looking at other athletes who are in even greater difficulty
  * holding a few short conversations here and there
  * observing the spectators' reactions
  * projecting your own finishing time
  * counting the number of athletes ahead of you at turning points
  * thinking of something pleasant, something that makes you happy

▲ Regeneration begins after you have run through the finish, in the form of light walking and stretching exercises. Put on dry clothing. It's time to start with the intake of food and drink. Shower, maybe a massage and a lot of conversation.

▲ When back at home take a relaxing bath. Next day go for a relaxed cycle, swim or run.

The Six Steps Of Running Training

I have staggered the training plans below as follows:

Step	Percentage of max. pulse	Kind of Training	Training Description	Example - max. pulse 175	Example - max pulse 165
1	60-70%	Recovery, easy training	Regeneration training; long slow runs	105-122	99-116
2	70-75%	Calm training	Basic endurance	122-131	116-124
3	75%	Relaxed training	Basic endurance	131	124
4	75-80%	Brisk training	Continuous run •	131-140	124-132
5	80-85%	Very brisk (fast) training	Fartlek e.g. e.g. 2-3 x 3miles/min	140-149	132-140
6	85-90%	Hard training	Tempo continuous run, half marathon, marathon	149-158	140-148
7	100%	Competition	5 000m competition	175	165

Training Step 1

60-70% of one's maximum pulse. Recovery training without much effort.

▲ Regeneration training up to 45 minutes

▲ Long, slow runs

▲ Fat burning area

For a regenerative continuous run, one runs at the lowest training speed. It's not the heart rate that's important here, but rather the active exercise, whereby e.g., lactate is broken down more effectively than at rest. Short runs are only carried out as a means of recovery following hard training or after competition.

Long continuous runs at a low running speed serve to improve and optimize long-term endurance. This is a vital basic element for triathletes wishing to go for the Ironman distance, as the important fat-burning is schooled here.

Training Step 2

70-75% of one's maximal pulse. **Calm training.**

The most frequent training takes place during steps 2,3 & 4, (at least four fifths of training volume for Masters), Decisive factors for ambitious athletes are endurance loads over several hours at these levels of intensity. These levels of intensity are the most important for working on one's basic endurance. Calm training means that one is constantly able to hold a conversation and take in the surrounding countryside.

Very well trained athletes complete their long, slow runs at these levels in a time of 2-2.5 hours.

Training Step 3

75% of one's maximum pulse. **Relaxed training**

The same commentary notes as for Step 2.

Heart rate measurements here have two important functions. On the one hand they ensure a rise in one's pulse limit and on the other hand they serve as a motivator when the speed gets too slow. However, one must remember that the correct heart rates don't indicate the actual load intensity until after the warm-up phase, i.e. after about 10-15 minutes.

Training Step 4

75-80% of one's maximum pulse. **Brisk training.**

This step is for practicing the brisk continuous run.

Load duration up to 90 minutes.

Endurance reaches a higher level in the process.

Training Step 5

80-85% of one's maximum pulse. **Fast training (very brisk).**

This rather exertive training is suitable for ambitious athletes; this takes up a small proportion of training. This depends on one's training state, training period and age.

e.g.   a 45-year-old newcomer: 1 x every two weeks

a 45-year-old experienced,   1 x weekly

ambitious athlete.

a 65-year-old experienced athlete: 1-2 x every two weeks.

One trains in aerobic/anaerobic metabolism at this training intensity. A continuous conversation is no longer possible for many athletes. At this level one carries out the longer continuous tempo runs in preparation for the marathon, such as 3 x 5 000m, 4 x 15 min, 2 x 30 min or 1 x 60 min. One can also bring in speed games (fartlek) at this level. Lactate rates are approx. 2.5 mmol/l. This step is for improving one's basic endurance ability as well as one's aerobic endurance ability. At the same time our muscular system gets used to the higher running speed and is better able to adapt.

Training Step 6

85-90% of one's maximum pulse. **Hard training**, continuous tempo run, competition training, half-marathon, marathon.

Running speeds in training are (damned) hard at this level, whereas in competition they are 'only' taxing due to our body's rested condition and our special motivation. Masters should train at this level only in the run-up to competitions over a period of about eight weeks and once a week at the very most. Younger Masters are obviously better able to cope with these hard training sessions of 5-6 x 1,000m, 3 x 2,000m, 4 x 2,000m or 3 x 3,000m than the slightly older Masters.

One also reaches these levels through fartlek methods. The rewarding break between the intervals should be extended until one's heart rate has fallen to at least 110, and for the older Masters to under 100 beats per minute.

Experienced triathletes can run their half-marathon at this level of intensity (90%), and their marathon at a slightly lower level (85-88%).

The pulse measurer has an important regulatory function here.

This form of training is for;
- ▲ improving one's performance capacity specifically for competition.
- ▲ improving one's lactate tolerance (increasing lactate buffer).
- ▲ getting used to competition speed.

As I personally dislike this form of hard training I have discovered two possible ways for this training to be enjoyable now and then.
- ▲ Being accompanied by a suitable training partner.
- ▲ The start on a people's race. The competitive motivation alone makes it much easier for me to practice this type of training.

Forms of Running Training

Building up One's Basic Endurance with Long, Slow Runs

Long slow runs are of crucial importance for triathletes. Together with long, calm cycling trips they are *the* training sessions for a successful finish in the longer triathlon distances. They create the necessary requirements for success on the long competitive routes, the half-distance or the Ironman distance. These long, slow runs considerably help us to improve our long-term endurance and without this we will not hold out in competitions that can go on for between four and fifteen hours. An athlete who tries to complete such competitions over 100 km with brisk training sessions only, may manage the swimming and cycling parts, but lacks experience in long runs for the last part.

A long continuous run is at least 100 minutes in duration and is relatively low in intensity (two thirds of maximum pulse). If it goes on for more than 2 hours one should aim for 60% of one's maximum pulse. An athlete who does not use a pulse measurer in training should select the speed for his long runs where he runs 100-150 seconds more slowly than in a marathon.

This can mean: if you run a marathon in 3:30h then the long, slow runs should be no faster than:

2:35 - 2:48 over 16 miles
2:54 - 3:09 over 18 miles
3:03 - 3:19 over 19 miles
3:12 - 3:29 over 20 miles

The general rule however is: better to be a little slower than to be too fast. It must be possible to hold a conversation over the entire distance. It is our muscles' ability to adapt that's important here and not our speed!

During these long runs our body burns up mostly fat, sparing our limited glycogen reserves at the same time. As energy production from our fatty acids is twice as high as from our carbohydrates and proteins, considerably more oxygen is needed for this process. This is only possible with a low running intensity.

Our body's reserves of carbohydrates hold out for up to 20 miles, depending on food intake before the competition. You should often try to get to this limit when running, but without reaching a state of exhaustion. This is how a long, slow run be-

Table of times for long, slow runs:

Marathon in hours	Marathon in min per mile	Long, slow runs in min per miles	Long, slow run; 16 miles in hours	Long slow run; 18 miles in hours	Long slow run; 19 miles in hours	Long, slow run; 20 miles in hours
2:59	6:50	8:30 - 9:20	2:16 - 2:30	2:33 -2:48	2:41 - 2:57	2:50 - 3.06
3:16	7:30	9:10 - 10:00	2:27- 2:40	2:45 - 3:00	2:54 - 3:10	3:03 - 3.20
3:30	8:00	9:40 - 10:30	2:35 -2:48	2:54 - 3:09	3:03 - 3:19	3:12 - 3:29
4:09	9:30	11:10-12:00	3:00- 3:12	3:22 -3:30	18 miles	18 miles in
					3:22 - 3:30	3:22 - 3:30

comes a crucial supporting factor for Masters in the preparation period.

These long, slow runs not only work on our fat burning but also on our muscles' ability to contract over a long period of time and to consume oxygen more effectively. This occurs through a rise in the number of small blood vessels and mitochondria in our active muscular system. The **mitochondria** as we know, are the 'mini power stations' in our body and ensure that our general performance capacity is improved (with this form of training we move up from a 2-cylinder motor to a 12-cylinder one).

Let's go back to the glycogen reserves. As these are limited, our body's metabolism increasingly switches over to energy production through fat burning. Inexperienced athletes feel this around the 19 mile mark when they 'hit the wall'. This means that they must reduce their speed, as the body has switched over to fat metabolism and more oxygen is required for this. It's only possible when running speed is reduced.

Experienced runners avoid this problem by running from the very beginning at a speed at which their mixed metabolism (i.e. from glycogen and fat) is immediately activated. In this way they can stretch out their limited glycogen reserves right up until the finishing line. This can be practiced with long, slow runs as our muscles learn not to tire out so soon. This similarly holds for the long cycles later on in this book.

Furthermore we can practice fluid intake on these long runs.

I take a detailed look at the mental attitude for long running and triathlon distances at a later stage in this book. One thing though, if our head hasn't got the right attitude, our legs won't be much better. In addition to the long time factor, certain unexpected problems can be recognised or guessed at in training. Included here are: a balanced strength allocation, the 'bite your teeth together' feeling for the last few miles, overcoming some 'lows', solving or holding out some unexpected problems such as when shoes suddenly start rubbing, socks and jerseys begin to chafe, unsuitable clothing etc.

Many of these possible inconveniences, which often mean failure in competition, also occur during these long runs, so one reacts appropriately to these matters. The old rule still holds for the marathon: the marathon itself doesn't begin until mile number 20.

For any athlete preparing for the triathlon distances, and who wishes to run a preparation marathon in spring at the end of his winter training, I can only recommend the following: do a total of six long, slow runs covering 16, 18, 19 and 20 mile running distances (one long, slow run a week) when you are not able to go on long cycles. If you are already doing regular long cycling training for 4-5 hours, then 4-5 long runs are enough. Experienced Masters can often manage it with four long runs.

Triathletes weighing more than 187,4lbs should make do with four long runs (3 hours maximum) and go on long, calm cycling trips instead:

Brisk endurance training can be carried out for up to 90 minutes. The general rule is:

The longer the training session, the slower you run.
The shorter the training session, the faster you can (don't have to) run!

Speed Endurance Training

Fartlek - continuous tempo run

Fartlek (speed games) – better known as **'child's play'** – as a short continuous tempo run!

If you ever watch children at play, there's one thing you notice immediately:

Children move around at various different speeds - they run calmly, briskly, quickly, they sprint and trot. This type of running is exactly what fartlek is all about, we should really call it 'child's play'.

If however we take a look at runners who wish to improve their running speeds, they do their rounds in a stadium, run measured distances on country roads or take the familiar forest route. If possible always the same training session, always this same running plan, always this same route, always the same people, the same topics of conversation etc. The epitome of monotony. It is possible to break this boredom in a playful, childlike manner and thus make running training interesting again. Let's do what children do. Let's play with speed in training.

We start off after a warm-up phase. Sprint along a distance of 80-120yds, build in quick sessions for 1-3 minutes or fast stages lasting more than 3 minutes. Between these fast sections, trot along easily for a particular period of time (you decide for how long). These little games can also be carried out in a group, in such a way that everyone has a turn in suggesting, e.g. accelerate as far as - the next house, the end of the forest, to the next tree, or whatever mark you may choose. After this fast running section comes calm, recovery running or even trotting. Load and recovery must also be in the correct proportion to each other when playing such speed games, in order for training to lead to improvements in performance.

When you feel like doing it again the whole procedure starts off anew. You yourself determine the speed. Fartlek is thus intensive,

does not involve pressure, and running distances and speeds are not laid down beforehand. A triathlete just runs as fast as he feels like doing on that particular day. Fartlek implies speed work which is playful and creative. Another great advantage of this childlike method is that you don't require a specific measured distance or a 400m running lane to do it.

Fartlek finishes off with easy cool-down running and light stretching exercises.

Continuous Tempo Run

The so-called **continuous tempo run** for our half marathon and marathon is based on our individual realistic competition times.

Any athlete wanting to have a go at these runs should possess a sufficient level of basic endurance. Continuous tempo runs last for 15 - 60 minutes depending on demand (10 miles, 26 miles) and performance capacity. They are carried out at a steady pace at approximately 85% of one's maximum pulse thus putting our aerobic/anaerobic mixed metabolism under demand. Pulse measurement is particularly important here: for actually reaching one's desired heart rate on the one hand, and for preventing it from going above this level on the other. It is advisable to carry out such runs on a route as even as possible. Suitable training partners are also a help as it easier to run within a group than to try and crack this tough nut by oneself. The continuous tempo run complies with the competition speed for a marathon.

It should take up a small part of one's training plan. 1 x a week at the most for Masters who are able ro run a marathon in 3:15h or faster. Those who take 3:30h or longer may run at his competition speed 2x a week for 30-60 minutes.

Tempo Training - Intervals

As opposed to the continuous methods, whereby one's speed is kept as constant as possible throughout the entire run or cycle, and the run comes complete with warm-up and cool-down phases, interval runs can be characterized by the planned alternation between load and recovery phases. The recovery phases, also referred to as **rewarding breaks**, do not go as far as a stage of complete regeneration. Depending on interval lengths they last for several minutes. An important factor is our heart rate here. Whereas well-trained athletes can take these rewarding breaks until a heart rate of 120 is reached, we Masters should extend these breaks until we have a heart rate of under 100, the younger Masters among us under 110. These runs are carried out in the area of the anaerobic threshold.

In order to achieve improvement over the 5,000m, 10,000m, half-marathon and marathon distances, the following continuous tempo runs or intervals can be recommended for Masters.

Suitable Intervals and Continuous Tempo runs for improving Running Times

Amount	Interval length (in m)	Speed	Particularly suitable for the following distances
4-8	1,000	10,000m tempo (TT)	5km, 10km, Marathon
2-4	2,000	10,000m tempo (TT)	5km, 10km, Marathon
2-3	3,000	10,000m tempo or Marathon tempo (MT)	10km, Marathon
2-3	5,000	Marathon tempo (MT)	Half-marathon, Marathon
1	1 hour	Marathon tempo (MT)	Marathon

TT: 10 kilometer running tempo

MT: Marathon running tempo

How often one uses these methods depends on one's state of performance, performance capacity and age. More details on this can be found in the training recommendations.

Runs /cycles with speed changes:

For any athlete who enjoys playing with speed when running or cycling, there is a further option - runs or cycles with speed changes. They can be built into almost every endurance training session. Following a warm-up phase, one runs or cycles for 6 x 2 minutes at a load of 85 -90%. You trot again in between until you have recovered.

Crescendo

Athletes who love training with variety will also occasionally enjoy frequently changing their running speeds. Choose a 3-5km long run and start off at a calm speed, then move up to a relaxed, then to a brisk, up as far as a fast load intensity. So you're going from 70% to 75%, then up to 80% and 85% of your maximum pulse. I personally like taking a 4km route for this and then complete it 4 times. As long as I feel good, I don't mind my heart rate approaching the 90% mark.

Hill Training

Be careful here: you quickly enter the anaerobic area doing hill training. Suitable for hill training is a gradient of 10-13% over a distance of 500 - 600yds. You run up the hill on the balls of your feet with a shortened stride. Up at the top you ease off gently for 500yds and then trot back down again.

Speed endurance training starts off with 3-4 hill runs, adding one more every week. As well as speed endurance you are also working on your strength endurance here.

Best Time over 10,000m

For keen and ambitious triathletes, who have a special prefer- ence for running or have changed over from running to triathlon, it is often just interesting to know: "In what time can I manage the 10 000m distance at the moment?" Furthermore, this running time also provides important information as regards one's possibilities with the half-distance marathon and marathon distances. I too was greatly fascinated by this distance. It was only when I surpassed my' dream time' that my motivation to improve my running time came to an abrupt stop. In running terms a 10,000m run refers to a stadium run, a 10km distance however is a road run.

I do not differ between a lane run and road run in the following explanations. There are several possibilities available to us triath- letes when attempting to complete the 10km distance as quickly as possible. As we are not merely runners, we cannot prepare for our best running time through pure running training.

I personally see two excellent opportunities for us to achieve a good 10km time:
▲ In connection with training for a spring or autumn marathon.
▲ As a finish off to the triathlon season.

In both cases it is possible to reach a good time for 10km with the help of a few, very fast training sessions. These 4-6 training sessions can be introduced 1 x a week. Warm-up and cool-down running are obviously also on the agenda here.

Week	Amount	Interval length (m)	Tempo	Trotting pause	Comments
1	5	1,000	TT	5-6 min	
2	3	2,000	TT + 5 s	10 min	
3	6	1,000	TT	5-6 min	
4	4	2,000	TT + 5 s	10 min	
Perhaps 5	8	1,000	TT + 5 s	5-6 min	
Perhaps 6	5	1,000	TT	5-6 min	

TT: desired 10km time

e.g. 40 min, i.e. 4:00 min/km

e.g. 45 min, i.e. 4:40 min/km

e.g. 50 min, i.e. 5:00 min/km

e.g. 55 min, i.e. 5:30 min/km

10 hints here:

▲ The intervals should be carried out in a relatively rested state.

▲ Pick out a suitable training partner for these quite hard runs.

▲ Run the intervals in your competition shoes.

▲ If it's too hard for you, then replace a session with an extensive fartlek instead.

▲ Basic training, i.e. the relaxed continuous runs, must not be neglected.

▲ The last tempo run should take place at least five days before competition.

▲ Only run for a good time when you feel top fit healthwise.

▲ In competition, make an absolute effort to run at a steady speed.

▲ If running with a pulse measurer, you may reach 95% of your maximum pulse. However only from km 3 to km 8 inclusively. After this your muscular system decides how fast you can run then.

▲ A marathon runner is also well able to complete a quick 10km run two weeks before or after the marathon run itself.

So now back to the practicalities. The upcoming information and statistics below show my attempt to run 10,000m within a good time.

Period: September, i.e. having finished the triathlon season.

Half-distance Marathon Training

An athlete wishing to take part in the Triathlon half-distance, swims 1.9 - 2.5km, cycles 56 miles and finally runs a half-distance marathon. Running is the toughest and most difficult of all three disciplines here as well. Whoever wishes to successfully run this half-distance marathon can only do this with appropriate running training. He won't manage this half-distance marathon by simply doing 10km running training. But, if he builds several 90-120 min long runs into his training schedule, he has a good chance of pulling through. Marathon training with appropriate long running sessions is definitely particularly suitable for completing the half-distance marathon.

An athlete who is training specifically for the half-distance and who has never participated in a marathon must heed the following advice:

You are on the best way to becoming a marathon runner with a run covering 13 miles. However this is not a must. A triathlete whose aim is to participate in several half-distances does not necessarily have to set his sights on the Ironman. But let's be honest, whoever takes part in so many so-called **half-distances** in triathlon, is generally on his way towards the Ironman distance. This way is also the right one and has proved itself to the utmost in sporting practice.

Half-distance marathon training for keen and ambitious Masters may not only consist of pure endurance training, it ought to (but doesn't have to) contain some fast and very fast low-distance runs for improving one's running abilities. Any triathlete planning a half-distance in the medium term should enter a good few half-distance marathons beforehand so as to lose any inhibitions or even fears he may have regarding the last discipline.

One can take part in a half-distance marathon both to finish off a short triathlon season as well as in spring in preparation for the upcoming half-distance triathlon.

An athlete who is in good health and has successfully completed a number of short triathlons, already fulfils the requirements necessary for participating in a half-distance marathon. Age is not a limit here. We all know just how many Masters entered their first half-distance marathon or marathon at an advanced age. And this they did without any injuries, on the contrary. With sensible training, the half-distance marathon is something worth aiming for, and is a good basis for managing the middle triathlon distance.

You are familiar with runs of 8-10 miles from training for the short triathlon. You're only missing several long runs for 90-120 minutes. For most athletes it's not the length of the distance, but rather the running speed that's the problem. The running speed really has to be slow and this is very difficult for many athletes. It's often the case that the quickest in the group determines the tempo and everyone else just runs along behind him, and continues doing so without a word of complaint. Nobody wants to show his true colors and break away, so they all just bite their teeth together and hold on till the bitter end - mmhh, and that's the end of another long, slow run. Stick to your guns and use your pulse

measurer as a rough guide; that's one possibility. Another possibility would be to pick out a slower runner than yourself, run 8 or 10 miles together and then you add on another calm run at the end. Just as possible, get your wife/partner or children to accompany you on their bike. Now you needn't have a guilty conscience about your long absence from home and even more, you have the opportunity to talk to each other.

Keen runners can work out a realistic finishing time for the half-distance marathon using a simple formula from the 10km run. This is as follows:

10km time x 2.222 = possible running time for the half-distance marathon.

e.g. You are able to run 10km within 50 minutes. Thus the possible running time for 13 miles would then be about 50 min x 2.222 = 111.1 min = 1.51h.

You can orient yourself around this time. External conditions naturally play an important role as well. However you cannot take account of these factors beforehand.

For a marathon runner, a suitable time for adding on a half-distance marathon to his schedule is four weeks before a marathon.

Two-month plan for a half-distance marathon in spring

This is what a two-month preparation period for a half-distance marathon in spring could look like: Swimming training and the occasional cycles which may occur, depending on weather conditions, are not specially listed.

Week Nr	Mon free	Tues- fast sections; 80-85%	Wed - free	Thurs - relaxed 75%	Fri - free	Sat - longer run 65-70%	Sun - relaxed 75%, perhaps cycling
1		60 min with fartlek		65min		70 min	45 min
2		3 x 1 000m, TT, in/out		45 min		10 km competition	2 hours cycle
3 Reg.		50 min with fartlek		45 min		50 min	30 min
4		70 min, 2 x 5 000m, HMT		60 min		90 min	45 min
5		60 min 4 x 1 000m TT		45 min		10 km competition	2 hours cycle
6 Reg		60 min with fartlek		40 min		60 min	30 min
7		85 min 3 x 4 000m, HMT		60 min		90 min	45 min
8		60 min with fartlek		80 min		70 min	35 min
9		60 min 3 x 1 000 in TT		30 min		Half-distance marathon competition	1-2 hours cycle

Explanation of training instructions:

TT: 1,000m sections at 10km running speed with a trotting break each time until pulse is < 110.

HMT: 4,000m or 5,000m sections at half-distance marathon speed with a 10 min trotting break each time until pulse is < 110.

Reg:	Regeneration week
Mondays:	No training
Tuesdays:	Fartlek. The runner determines the number, length and speed of the fast sections by himself. During the regeneration weeks only short, fast sections.
Wednesdays:	No training.
Thursdays	Relaxed training (75%), 15 min ABC run.
Fridays:	No training.
Saturdays:	Long continuous runs (65-70%), 15 min ABC run.
Sundays:	Relaxed: Calm cycles, pedalling frequency 90-100 revolutions per minute. If the weather is bad then postpone.

Training days and sessions can of course be switched around, even Sat. and Sun.

1-2 x a week ABC run, i.e. carry out three sequences of the following exercises over 10-30m for each of the following exercises: skipping, walking with your heels, knees-up running, running with little jumps, jump and run.

Depending on ambition level, skill and will, one can of course alter these training plans. The important thing always is that each athlete adjusts them to fit in with his own individual situation.

How To Best Manage the Half-Distance Marathon

The half-distance marathon is by no means a walkover, it demands the steadiest possible running speed. Many athletes tear away at the beginning as if it were a 10km run. The dramatic end comes at the 10-mile mark at the latest.

From my experience I would say that the half-distance marathon can be run at a heart rate of 90% of one's maximum pulse. Experienced Masters can even run it at rates of 90-92%. I would recommend beginners and older Masters to be more careful here - a considerably lower number of beats per minute is enough for them.

One thing is very important however. One's heart rate under exercise does not actually set in until the second mile onwards. Similarly, you shouldn't pay any more attention to your pulse measurer for the final two miles either, as your heart rate rises due to body warming at this stage.

Marathon - a Cornerstone for the Middle and Ironman Distances

Running is the most difficult discipline for the majority of triathletes, particularly for those athletes who have changed over to triathlon from other endurance sports (swimming, cycling). But even for triathletes who originally stem from the running scene there is a number of facts about triathlon running which distinguish it from running as a discipline of its own. This is particularly true for the Ironman triathlon.

I would like to differentiate between a marathon run and an Ironman marathon in the following table:

Differences between a Marathon and an Ironman Marathon

Marathon	Ironman Marathon
One goes to the start in a rested state.	One starts here having done 2.4 miles swimming and 112 miles on the bike in a considerably tired state, both physically and mentally.
Due to the calculable duration of competition, one can easily estimate weather conditions.	Adaptation to changing weather conditions is only possible to a limited extent, as the Ironman begins at 7 in the morning. The running section however doesn't begin until the afternoon and often doesn't finish until it's dark.
With appropriate warm-up the runner finds his running rhythm immediately.	The transition from the long cycle to running makes it more difficult to find the right running rhythm.
It is possible to plan running speed relatively exactly, even when taking account of the prevailing weather conditions.	Planning of running speed is only possible to a limited extent due to the exertion up to now.
It is possible to run on past the 3km mark with a given heart rate.	Even at the beginning of the run, one must take not only one's heart rate into consideration, but also the strain on one's support and locomotor apparatus as well as on one's muscles.

Body signals are only evident at a later stage in the marathon. This generally occurs in the final third of the run.

The exertion up to now demands a 'sensitive' transition from cycling to running as well as early perception of body signals.

Intake of food and drink can be planned exactly.

Intake of food and drink must be significantly more extensive.

The optimal running shoe can be lighter.

A different form of strain on the leg muscles during the cycling section affects our running technique. This means that a more stable shoe is required.

It is possible, after dropping out of the run, to make a new start within a short time, which makes up for the negative experience.

Due to the long duration of competition, the psychological strain is higher, and therefore the mental attitude is much more important than for a normal marathon. Dropping out at this stage can trigger off long-term frustration as one is often only able to take a second try a year later. Weak running performance - when one is overtaken by many athletes - can have a demoralizing and wearing effect, is then more likely to lead to a drop-out.

Because of the reasons mentioned above, running training for an Ironman competition is of utmost importance. In order to combat the *Marathon* mental barrier, I can only seriously recommend every aspiring Ironman to take part in a marathon during the preparation period. Needless to say, an athlete who wishes to enter a competition in the middle distance, will be able to pull through with much fewer risks better when he too completes a marathon run beforehand.

More advanced Masters (the older Masters among us) obviously must measure out their dosage of training carefully as regeneration simply takes longer. Training must not become too exertive. Experienced Masters are often keen competitors, and instead of the brisk and fast continuous tempo runs and intervals in training, are better taking part in competitions. I too belong to this category of runners. I find runs in training at marathon tempo (MT) covering distances of 2-3 x 5,000m or 6 x 1,000m at 10km tempo (TT) relatively difficult. However I find running at the same speed in a people's run or fun run much easier, without having to overexert myself.

Masters are well able to cope with long, continuous runs and these are an absolute must on the training agenda.

There are two reasons why it can be a good idea for Masters to do *block training* when preparing for a Middle and/or Ironman Distance. This means doing emphasis training in either swimming, cycling or running for four weeks in each case, and neglecting the other two disciplines in the process. Firstly, the snow and ice during the winter months can spoil every triathlete's training on the bike, and secondly Masters need a longer transitional or major regeneration period when they should, and must, recover from the exertions of the previous year, in order to start off the new year fully regenerated and ready to try their luck with new heroic sporting deeds again. Block training has proved to be worthwhile for *getting into gear* more quickly here.

One can recommend block training, which starts off e.g. in February with the swimming block, while also increasing basic endurance training for running; the actual running block itself comes in March with the first few cycles before moving on to the cycling block in April with reduced swimming and running training. One can then plan a marathon run for the beginning or middle of April. For those who start out into the triathlon season at a later stage, a very good time for a marathon is directly after the cycling block. The long endurance trips on the bike also accommodate every athlete during a marathon - they are simply kinder to one's joints, tendons and muscles than the long runs covering 19-20 miles.

Which running times can I manage in a Marathon race?

The question of a realistic marathon finishing time is very important for a concrete planning of training, as this speed has to be 'learned' regularly in training. The answer depends on a lot of factors e.g. basic speed, training volume and intensity, talent, willpower, mental attitude among many others. Basically all those things I mentioned with the runner's overall situation.

Three factors provide clear assistance when answering the question about one's potential marathon finishing time:
1. Competition finishing times achieved while preparing for the marathon.
2. Running feeling.
3. Heart rates.

Competition Times Achieved in the Run-up to a Marathon

Working towards a particular marathon finishing time is quite motivating for most runners. One is just better able to train then. However the target time that one sets should be based on a realistic estimate. Particularly helpful here are the finishing times achieved in 10km and 13 mile competitions up to now. They provide us with useful information for our potential marathon running time. When tackling the tricky question about the finishing time one should aim for, I personally consider this information to be of vital importance along with running feeling and heart rates. With a good basic speed and the necessary endurance training, one definitely has an advantage over those with a lower basic speed. Assuming of course similar endurance ability.

Below is a table for determining one's **potential marathon running time** based on 10km and half-distance marathon times already achieved.

10km Target Time in Minutes	Corresponding 5,000m Time in Minutes	Corresponding 1,000m Time in Minutes (TT)	Half-Distance Marathon **Target Time** in Hours	**Potential Marathon Running Time in Hours**
35	17:30	3.30	1:18	2:43
36	18:00	3:36	1.20	2:48
37	18:30	3:42	1:22	2:53
38	**19:00**	**3:48**	**1:24**	**2:57**
39	19:30	3:54	1.27	3:02
40	20:00	4:00	1:29	3:07
41	20:30	4:06	1:31	3:11
42	21:00	4:12	1:33	3.16
43	21:30	4:18	1:36	3:21
44	22:00	4:24	1:38	3:25
45	**22:30**	**4:30**	**1:40**	**3:30**
46	23:00	4:36	1:42	3:35
47	23:30	4:42	1:44	3:39
48	24:00	4:48	1:47	3:44
49	24:30	4:54	1:49	3:49
50	25:00	5:00	1:51	3:53
51	25:30	5:06	1:53	3:58
52	26.00	5:12	1:56	4:03
53	26:30	5:18	1:58	4:07
54	**27.00**	**5.24**	**2:00**	**4:12**
55	27:30	5:30	2:02	4:17
56	28:00	5:36	2:04	4:21
57	28:30	5:42	2:07	4:26
58	29:00	5:48	2:09	4:31
59	29:30	5:54	2:11	4:36
60	30.00	6:00	2:13	4:40

The calculated values are based on the following formulae:

Half-distance marathon time   = 10km time x 2.222

Marathon time   = 10km time x 4.666 (alternatively 10km time x 14/3)

We can read the following from the table:

If we add five, six or seven minutes to the half-distance marathon time, this gives us the 13 mile passing time during the marathon.

Running Feeling

In the course of time, the more mature athlete develops the right 'feeling' for his body and for the right speed. Particularly helpful here is the use of pulse measuring devices during training, particularly when running in MT (marathon tempo).

Apart from both the running times achieved during marathon preparation and the appropriate heart rates, a runner's feeling is also a decisive factor for his success in a marathon. The necessary basis for this however must occur in training, as it's only here that one can develop a feeling for the right speed.

This happens principally during the continuous tempo runs, i.e. when one trains in MT (marathon tempo) for over an hour or when 3 x 5,000m in MT is on the agenda. After all, the desired running speed has to be kept up for three or four hours, and not just for one hour. Another crucial aspect is to run at a steady rhythm. The biggest mistake that you can make during a marathon, is to just tear away at the start and say to yourself "What's out of the way is out of the way!" You're certain to pay the penalty for this from about the 19th mile onwards. Every minute you had gained up to now slips away at five times the speed. We can learn again from the top-class runners. They can even manage to be one, two or three minutes faster on the second half of the marathon. The reason for this is quite simple. In this way they save their carbohydrate supplies at the beginning of the race and are able to draw on these reserves for the last few miles in the crucial phase of the run.

Heart Rates

It is possible to run a marathon at 85-88% of one's maximum heart rate. However this rate only holds from km 3 to 33! Beforehand, the heart rate is lower, and towards the end of the run it rises considerably again due to body warming. Newcomers are advised to stick to 85%; highly competitive and experienced marathon runners may approach the 88-90% mark of maximum pulse.

A marathon can be run with a lactate concentration of 2.0-2.5 mmol/l. An athlete who knows his exact heart rates for lactate levels of 2.0-2.5 mmol/l can try and reach these rates during a marathon. The 2.0 mmol/l lactate rate is more relevant for a three-minute load duration on the treadmill.

And now HAVE FUN with the challenge that you face i.e. to manage *forty-two thousand, one hundred and ninety-five meters*! With the right attitude and the correct tempo, a marathon can be a lot of fun. Remember, most people would be happy if they could have a go at this!

Marathon Training Plans - Working towards specific Finishing Times

As already mentioned in the previous chapter, the months of October (perhaps), and then November, December and January are the months of regeneration. During this transitional period keen and competitive Masters should follow up their four-week training vacuum in which only sporadic training took place, with two relaxed runs per week, 1-2 swimming sessions and the odd cycling session.

You could also plan on the following:

February, the swimming month: three swimming, three running and occasional cycling sessions. One must prepare for the running month here.
March, the running month: four running, 1-2 swimming and 1-2 cycling sessions.

April, the cycling month: 3-4 cycling, 1-2 swimming and 2 running sessions of training.

You could enter the marathon run in the first week in April, i.e. the week following the running block or at the end of April, when most marathons take place in the first instance. The end of April is right in the middle of the cycling block, but this should not pose a problem for a triathlete. In the week before the marathon, he should only carry out very gentle, regenerative cycling training as well as 1-2 'calm-down' runs. The cycling block should then be extended by a week.

A pure running training plan is not the important thing for a triathlete, but rather a schedule combining all three endurance sports in the preparation period. This means that after the regenerative months, we have February, March and April to prepare specifically for the marathon.

Plan 1: Target Marathon Finish: 4:12h

Requirements: 10km in 54 min.(TT 05:24 min/km)
Half-distance marathon in 2:00h
Marathon tempo (MT) = 9:38 min/mile
Fartlek (FL)

Weeks 1-12	Running Training	Swimming Training	Cycling Training	Comments
1 February	1 x 11miles relaxed 1 x 8 miles with FL 10km competition (90%)	Swimming block - three sessions per week	Occasional Cycles in February	**Swimming Block 3 x S**

2 February	1 x 11 miles relaxed 1 x 8miles with FL 1 x 16 miles very calm	As above	As above	As above
3 February	1 x 11 miles relaxed 1 x 8 miles with FL 16 miles very calm	As above	As above	As above
4 February	1 x 11 miles relaxed 1 x 8 miles with FL. **10km competition (90%)**	As above	As above	As above
5 March	1 x 11 miles relaxed 1 x 8 miles with FL 1 x 1h MT 16 miles very calm	1-2 swimming sessions	1-2 cycling trips, easy pedalling	**Running Block 3 x R**
6 March	1 x 11 miles relaxed 1 x 8 miles with FL. 1x 1h MT. 18 miles very calm	As above	As above	As above

7 March	1 x 11 miles calm. 1 x 8 miles relaxed. 1 x 4 x 1,000m TT **Half-distance marathon in 2:00**	As above	As above	As above
8 March	1 x 11 miles relaxed 1 x 8 miles with brisk sections. 16 miles very calm	As above	As above	As above
9 April	1 x 9 miles relaxed 1 x 1h MT 1 x 16 miles calm	1 x swimming session	4 x cycling training	**Cycling Block 3 x C**
10 April	1 x 8 miles relaxed Tues/Wed 3.000m (MT) **Marathon**	1 x swimming session	3 x cycling training, relaxed	As above
11 April	3 x relaxed cycling sessions, 1 x continuous swim, 1 x running			
12 April	4 x cycling training, 1-2 swimming training, 2 x relaxed running training			

May   Combination/Transition Training

Please don't forget to adhere to the most important training principles (Chapter 10). After the marathon run you have a 3-week regeneration phase!

Plan 2: Target Marathon Finish: 3:31h

Requirements: 10km in 45 min (TT = 4:30h)
Half-distance marathon in 1:40h
Marathon tempo (MT) = 8:00 min/mile
Fartlek (FL)

Weeks 1-12	Running Training	Swimming Training	Cycling Training	Comments
1 February	1 x 11 miles relaxed 1 x 8 miles with FL 10km competition (90%)	Swimming block, three training sessions a week	In February occasional cycling	**Swimming Block 3 x S**
2 February	1 x 11 miles relaxed, 1 x 8 miles with FL 1 x 16 miles very calm	As above	As above	As above
3 February	1 x 11 miles relaxed 1 x 8 miles with FL 16 miles very calm	As above	As above	As above
4 February	1 x 11 miles relaxed 1 x 8 miles	As above	As above	As above

with FL
**10km
competition (95%)**

5 March	1 x 11 miles calm 1 x 8 miles with FL 1 x 1h MT 17 miles very calm	1-2 swimming sessions	1-2 cycling trips, easy pedalling	**Running Block 4 x R**
6 March	1 x 11miles relaxed 1 x 8 miles with FL 1 x 1 h MT 17 miles very calm	As above	As above	As above
7 March	1 x 11 miles calm 1 x 8 miles relaxed 1 x 5 x 1000m TT Half-distance marathon in 1:40h	As above	As above	As above
8 March	1 x 6 miles calm. 1 x 11 miles relaxed 1 x 8 miles with brisk sections. 1 x 16 miles very calm	As above	As above	As above

9 April	1 x 9 miles relaxed 1 x 1h MT 1 x 16 miles calm	1 x swimming session	4 x cycling training	**Cycling Block 3-4 x C**
10 April	1 x 8 miles, relaxed Tues/Wed 3,000m MT **Marathon**	1 x swimming session	3 x cycling training, relaxed	As above
11 April:	3 x relaxed cycling sessions, 1 x continuous swim, 1 x running			
12 April	4 x cycling training, 1-2 x swimming training, 2 x relaxed running training			

May: Combination/Transition Training

Please don't forget to adhere to the most important training principles (Chapter 10). After the marathon you have a 3-week regeneration phase!

Plan 3: Target Marathon Finish: 3:15h

Requirements: 10km in 42 min (TT = 4:12 min/km)
                Half-distance marathon in 1:33 h
                Marathon tempo(MT) = 7:28 min/mile
                Fartlek FL

Weeks 1-12	Running Training	Swimming Training	Cycling Training	Comments
1 February	1 x 11 miles relaxed 1 x 8 miles with FL **10km competition (90%)**	Swimming block 3 sessions per week	In February occasional cycling trips	**Swimming block 3 x S**
2 February	1 x 11 miles relaxed 1 x 8 miles with FL. 1x16 miles very calm	As above	As above	As above
3 February	1 x 11 miles relaxed. 1x 8 miles with FL 16 miles very calm	As above	As above	As above
4 February	1 x 11 miles relaxed 1 x 8 miles with FL. **10 km competition (95%)**	As above	As above	As above

5 March	1 x 11 miles calm 1 x 8 miles with Fl 1 x 1h MT 18 miles very calm	1-2 swimming sessions	1-2 cycling sessions easy pedalling	**Running Block** **4 x R**
6 March	1 x 11 miles relaxed 1 x 8 miles with FL 1 x 1h MT 17 miles very calm	As above	As above	As above
7 March	1 x 11 miles calm 1 x 8 miles relaxed 1 x 5 x 1.000m TT **Half-distance marathon in 1:33h**	As above	As above	As above
8 March	1 x 6 miles calm 1 x 11 miles relaxed 1 x 8 miles with brisk sections 1 x 16 miles very calm	As above	As above	As above

| 9 April | 1 x 8 miles relaxed
1 x 1h MT
1 x 16 miles calm | 1 x swimming session | 4 x cycling training | **Cycling block**
3-4 x C |
| 10 April | 1 x 8 miles relaxed
Tues/Wed
3,000m TT
Marathon | 1 x swimming session | 3 x cycling training relaxed | As above |

11 April: 3 x relaxed cycling sessions, 1 x continuous swim, 1 x running

12 April 4 x cycling training, 1-2 x swimming training, 2 x relaxed running training

May: Combination/Transition Training

Please don't forget to adhere to the most important training principles (Chapter 10). After the marathon you have a 3-week regeneration phase.

Plan 4: Target Marathon Finish: 2:59h

Requirements: 10km in 38:00 min (TT = 3:48 min/km)
                          Half-distance marathon in 1:24h
                          Marathon tempo (MT) = 6:50 min/mile
                          Fartlek

Weeks 1-12	Running Training	Swimming Training	Cycling Training	Comments
1 February	1 x 11 miles relaxed 1 x 8 miles with FL **10km competition (90%)**	Swimming block - three sessions per week	In February occasional cycling trips	**Swimming block 3-4 x S**
2 February	1 x 11 miles relaxed 1 x 8 miles with FL 1 x 16 miles very calm	As above	As above	As above
3 February	1 x 11 miles relaxed 1 x 8 miles with FL 16 miles very calm	As above	As above	As above
4 February	1 x 11 miles relaxed 1 x 8 miles	As above	As above	As above

with FL
10km competition
(95%)

Date				
5 March	1 x 11 miles calm 1 x 8 miles with FL 1 x 1h MT 18 miles very calm	1-2 swimming sessions	1-2 cycling trips, easy pedalling	**Running Block 4 x R**
6 March	1 x 11 miles relaxed 1 x 11 miles with FL 1 x 1h MT 17 miles very calm	As above	As above	As above
7 March	1 x 11 miles calm. 1x8 miles relaxed 1x 5x 1,000m TT **Half-distance Marathon in 1:24h**	As above	As above	As above
8 March	1 x 8 miles calm. 1x11 miles relaxed 1 x 8 miles with brisk sections 1 x 16 miles very calm	As above	As above	As above

9 April	1 x 9 miles relaxed 1 x 1h MT 1 x 16 miles calm	1 x swimming session	4 x cycling training	**Cycling block 3-4 x C**
10 April	1 x 8 miles, relaxed Tues/Wed 3,000m (TT) **Marathon**	1 x swimming session	3 x cycling training relaxed	As above

11 April 3 x relaxed cycling sessions, 1 x continuous swim, 1 x running

12 April 4 x cycling training, 1-2 x swimming training, 2 x relaxed running training

May Combination/Transition Training

Please don't forget to adhere to the most important training principles (Chapter 10). After the marathon you have a 3-week regeneration phase.

By taking account of the following age-group coefficients according to CEPELKA we end up with the following interesting statistics:

Age	Age Coefficient	2:40h	3:00h	3:20h	3:40h	4:00h
27	1.0000	2:40:00	3:00:00	3:20:00	3:40:00	4:00:00
30	0.9927	2:41:10	3:01:20	3:21:28	3:41:37	4:01:45
35	0.9690	2:45:07	3:05:46	3:26:24	3:47:02	4:07:40
40	0.9411	2:50:00	3:11:16	3:31:31	3:53:46	4:15:01
45	0.9132	2:55:20	3:17:06	3:39:01	4:00:54	4:22:49
50	0.8854	3:00:42	3:23:18	3:45:53	4:08:28	4:31:04
55	0.8575	3:06:35	3:29:55	3:53:14	4:16:54	4:39:52
60	0.8252	3:13:54	3:38:09	4:02:22	4:26:36	4:50:49
65	0.7817	3:24:41	3:50:16	4:15:51	4:41:22	5:07:01
70	0.7253	2:40:36	4:08:10	4:35:45	5:03:19	5:33:53

Running Performance over 26.2 miles According to Age

The following information can be read from this table: If an athlete at the age of 60 is able to run the marathon distance in 4:02h, his performance is comparable to a top class athlete who runs in a time of 3:20h.

A marathon finishing time of 3:00h achieved by an athlete aged 50 corresponds to a 2:40h running performance by a 26-27-year old top class runner. A running time of 4:50h by a sixty-year old athlete can be compared to a time of 4:01h by a 30-year old athlete.

An interesting and motivating numerical comparison for us Masters.

For which athletes is it a good idea to take part in a marathon at the end of the triathlon season?

a) For those athletes who have taken part in one or more Middle Triathlon competitions this year and are planning an Ironman distance for next year.
b) For those who simply enjoy running a marathon in a good time.
c) For those who are looking for a further sporting challenge following a short triathlon season.

To all these athletes I would like to say that the chances of achieving a good running time are excellent at the end of a triathlon season, provided one does not intend to lift the legalities of a marathon off their hinges. More details on this can be found earlier in this chapter.

Training switches around somewhat in favour of running, although one should still keep to one swimming session per week and a few calm cycling trips. Everyone is capable of getting to grips with the training schedules indicated and add in a running session with a little fartlek (FL). Be careful however: regeneration, the rest days in the week, must not be neglected. One should have at least two complete days of rest (from sport) a week, depending on age and experience.

We no longer need to discuss the effectiveness of cycling sessions during marathon preparation, having already seen the comparison of both training schedules (Plan 1 and 2). More details of this can be found in the next chapter, 'Cycling'.

Running: Regeneration and Winter Training

One distinguishing feature of running when compared with swimming and cycling is that it's a sport which can be carried out the whole year round. Whatever kind of weather we have - except for lightning and icy roads - running is possible everywhere. This also means that even during the transitional phase, i.e. the phase of major regeneration, one's basic endurance remains. Certainly it is also possible to go an entire month without running and do a little swimming or cycling so as not to lose track completely. A relaxed running session over one hour twice a week - those who like running may also go three times in the week - along with a single swimming session is very good for regeneration, and an athlete can already start forging plans for the next season. Long winter evenings together with the family are perfect for this task and feelings of anticipation about the oncoming warmer weather already set in.

However, I would like to warn against continuing with competition in autumn, in winter and in spring. An athlete who still takes part in several marathons in autumn, participates in all cross-country runs in winter and continues with marathon participation again in spring needn't be surprised when he is faced with a number of injuries and illnesses, not to mention a serious lack of enthusiasm. Masters simply require longer for regeneration and need more days of rest per week than a 20-30-year old athlete.

CHAPTER 5

Cycling

The Easy Discipline?

Every triathlete is able to ride a bike. That's fine, but there's a difference between cycling for 25 miles and 56 miles or even 112 miles. Bolting along until your thighs fall apart, this may be possible for an hour, but on the longer distances other stipulations hold. The right speed must be carefully selected, a speed which can be kept up as constantly as possible over a number of hours.

Another point here is that one still has to complete a long run afterwards. The combination of long swimming, cycling and running disciplines is what makes participation in the Middle and Ironman distances particularly appealing. It is a great challenge for every triathlete to have a go at and cope with these distances. Even after 30 Long and Ironman Distances, to take part in an Ironman triathlon is still something exceptional for me, something extremely special, something fantastic in my life. Something that you don't simply do with a snip of your fingers.

If we look at time distribution for the Middle and Ironman distances, the results are very interesting.

From the pure time aspect in the Middle and Triathlon Distances, one needs **11-14% for swimming, 52-55% for cycling and 31-36% for the running discipline**. Cycling takes up by far the largest amount of time in competition. Thus it is possible to gain or lose a lot of time while cycling.

In order for bike racing to be fun, one needs of course the appropriate bike. The typical triathlon bike has stood its own for the long and very long stretches in particular. Before I go on here though, a normal racing bike is certainly fine for some of the training distances. However one should ride the triathlon bike (the competition bike) regularly so as to be able to master it well in tricky competition situations, such as on steep uphill and downhill routes.

Cycling equipment and technique training is already dealt with in great detail in "Lifelong Success - Triathlon: Training for Masters." So not to have to repeat myself I would like to look at cycling training specifically for the Middle and Ironman distances.

As already mentioned in year planning, the racing distance of 90-180km requires training of great continuity. Many triathletes, however, live in regions where this continuity is only possible to a limited extent. Therefore one must look for and practice other training alternatives. These are illustrated in detail shortly.

General Distribution of Competition Times in the Middle and Ironman Distances

Distance (in miles)	Swimming Time in h	Cycling Time in h	Running Time in h	Total Time in h	Swimming Time in %	Cycling Time in %	Running Time in %
Middle							
1.2/56/13	0:40	2:40	1:30	4:50	14	55	31
Middle	0:46	3:00	1:40	5:26	14	55	31
Ironman							
2.4/112/26	0:50	4:20	2:48	7.58	11	54	35
Ironman	1:07	5:15	3:25	9:47	11	54	35
Ironman	1:15	5:48	4:00	11:03	11	53	36
Ironman	1:30	6:30	4:30	12:30	12	52	36
Ironman	1:55	7:30	5:00	14:25	13	52	35

The 56 and 112 mile cycling distances are virtually completed within the aerobic area, so appropriate training is required here too. The main training emphasis clearly revolves around basic endurance and this must be worked on the whole year round where possible. Several short, brisk training sequences are necesary for improving this basic endurance. Strength endurance is just as important for cycling. Cycling training includes those training forms and intensities explained below.

Regenerative Cycling Trips

Regenerative cycles are restful, easy-going training sessions. They are particularly suitable
- ▲ after competitions
- ▲ following high exertion in training e.g. long runs, intensive cycling training, during the running block, during the swimming block
- ▲ for the rare cycling tours in winter

Cycling trips at such low intensities (55-65%) ensure that recovery is enhanced. After long competitions the necessary regeneration takes place more quickly with such tours rather than through total inaction. So there, an easy-going trip on the bike which is not part of training ensures quicker regeneration than a lie-down on the sofa.

Fat Metabolism Training

Training within the fat metabolism phase is very important for athletes who wish to enter the Middle and Ironman Distances. As our stores of glycogen are limited, our fat reserves unlimited however, one just has to train for this. Fat metabolism occurs only at very low intensities, at 60-65% of one's maximum pulse. So it's a particularly good idea to know one's maximum heart rate when cycling too.

Fat metabolism training needs to go on for a duration of more than 2-3 hours. Because of the low orthopedic load on on our body while cycling, it is these long training cycling sessions which are suitable for exertions over a long period of time. One should try to reach a pedalling frequency of 100 revolutions per minute. Regular fat metabolism training enhances the growth in the number and size of our mitochondria, the mini-power stations in our muscles' cells. This training can bring us from being a two-cylinder motor up to a four-, six-, eight-, ten- or even twelve-cylinder motor.

Fat metabolism training is particularly effective on an empty stomach. An athlete who completes his cycling training at low intensity (60-65%) and doesn't begin with solid foods (banana, dried fruit, bread roll) until after two hours, can save himself many hours of training with this method.

I like to make use of this method on holiday. I get on my bike at 7 in the morning with an empty stomach, and I naturally have two large bottles of fluids with me. If hunger sets in, I have a banana and some dried fruit in my jersey. As I know that breakfast is on the table when I return from my two-and-a-half-hour cycling training, I nearly always manage to do without eating.

Basic Endurance

Basic endurance – the term speaks for itself. The basis for long endurance is what we are to work on here. Basic endurance forms the foundation for the brisk and fast training later on. You start off pedalling with the small gear and 100 revolutions at a level of intensity which is approx. 65-70 of your maximum pulse. For shorter trips of about an hour you may even go up to 75%. This form of training is not only to be used in the preparation period, but rather of the whole year round, as it is the platform for improvement in one's performance. With long, calm, relaxed rides for up to several hours, our endurance abilities are improved.

Anyone who does not know his highest cycling heart rate can look at the following chart as a guide. This shows the upper and lower heart rates according to age.

Development of **Basic Endurance for Masters while Cycling**

Age in Years	Load Duration up to 90 minutes	Load Duration up to 150 minutes	Load Duration over 150 minutes
40-50	130-145	125-140	120-135
50-60	125-140	120-135	115-130
Over 60	120-135	115-130	110-125

Speed Endurance Training - Fartlek on the Bike

As already mentioned in running training, fartlek is a varied form of training. Such speed games school your speed endurance and bring variety into training. It's also easy to carry out in a group.

Included here are the methods which I dealt with in detail in 'Lifelong Success - Triathlon: Training for Masters' such as the 'Place Name Sign' Test or 'Scooter' tests. Cycling within a group is another example of speed games. The cyclist at the front cycles at a high level of intensity whereas the cyclists toward the back cycle at a significantly lower level of intensity.

For triathletes who train by themselves a lot of the time, fartlek is a brief and interesting change from the long and very long cycling training sessions. Cycling at intensities of up to 85% of one's maximum heart rate involves a higher demand on our cardiovascular system and improves basic endurance. Having said this, Masters should not turn every cycling session into a speed game, as the intensity is too high for working on a solid basic endurance level. Speed endurance training or fartlek should appear 1x a week on the training schedule, in order to achieve an improvement in cycling performance.

Tempo Rides for 6, 12, 18 Miles

The first phase of the preparation period does not include tempo rides, as a solid foundation for basic endurance is required here. One hits the aerobic/anaerobic area during such intensive training sessions on the bike and for this reason one must use tempo rides carefully, according to performance ability and age. Helpful here is a small training group with a similar performance capacity. Each tempo ride begins and ends off with a relaxed cycle of 30 minutes. One cycles at an intensity of 80-85% of one's maximum heart rate.

The possibilities available when preparing for the Middle and Ironman Distances are:
▲ 3-5 x 6 miles with a break of 15 minutes easy pedalling each time
▲ 2-3 x 12 miles with a break of 20 minutes easy pedalling each time
▲ 1-2 x 18 miles with a break of 30 minutes easy pedalling

Younger Masters can include these long tempo sessions into their training schedules more frequently than the more mature Masters.

Strength Endurance Training

General strength endurance is built up at the same time as basic endurance when cycling. Mountain strength endurance training, however, should not take place in the first cycling weeks of the year, but only after several weeks of training. When cycling on hilly territory, strength endurance training occurs mostly on the uphill stretches, which can be cycled in a sitting position or in a rocking position. Top load levels can be as high as 90% of one's maximum pulse. The lactate in one's muscles can be broken down again on the descents or during the flat sections.

Anyone without long hills in the surrounding region can carry out strength endurance on even surfaces by using a high gear and only 70 revolutions per minute. What's important here is the warm-up and cool-down cycling periods.

The rule again for the more mature Masters among us: one doesn't have to keep up with the young athletes at every hill.

Cycling - Emphasis Training

Triathletes who are lucky enough to live in regions where conditions are favourable for cycling the whole year round, can choose between a continuous build-up of training or emphasis training in cycling. Because of the prevailing weather conditions, emphasis training (a cycling block) is better for many athletes. We can work on our basic endurance with weekly cycles that are long and calm. A lot of time is needed for this however. In order to cut down this time aspect, one should try and cycle to work where possible. One can nearly always manage to track down a shower and a cupboard with clothes to change into.

By taking appropriate detours on the way home, it is quite easy to 'stretch' the distances to the desired length.

Important: Before starting with emphasis training, be sure to check that the saddle is at the correct height. To do this, sit down on the bike with your running shoes on. One pedal is at its lowest position. The saddle is at the right height when your leg is outstretched and the heel of your shoe touches the pedal. Important! Don't slide down sideways from the saddle!

Cycling Month: An athlete who chooses a whole month for a cycling block should ensure that cycling training is on the agenda at least 4x a week. In addition to this 2x swimming and 2x running. As these training sessions take up a relatively large amount of time, it's advisable to work this out beforehand and see how it fits in with one's personal circumstances.

As regards intensity, the same rules hold for cycling as for running: the longer the distance, the lower the speed. When preparing for Ironman, a cycle once a week of well over 60 miles ought to be part of the training schedule. Perhaps it's possible to start off with 60 miles and increase this by 6 miles every week. Speed games are allowed on the shorter distances. Other than that, one practices round pedalling at 100-110 revolutions per minute, using the small chain gear.

It is also possible to structure cycling blocks for the weekends. On four weekends or on days off work we could have the following:

Week	Fridays miles	Saturdays miles	Sundays miles
1	50	56	62
2	56	62	68
3	62	68 + 3 miles run	75
4	68	56 + 5 miles run	80

Cycling Training 'Holidays'

Those athletes who don't have cycling opportunities during the transitional period and then complete a one- or two-week cycling block in southern regions in the preparation period should pay attention to the following aspects:

In the run-up to this emphasis on *cycling,* one should make use of every opportunity beforehand to cycle several hundred kilometers at least. Only then can one be sure that the extensive training in warmer climes will pay off.

This important training phase serves as basic training only, thus providing the basis for targeted training work shortly before and during the competition period. On long, calm trips lasting up to several hours it is mainly our endurance capacity that is improved, our metabolism is exercised. Low gears and pedalling frequencies of between 100 and 110 are important here. For this reason uphill stretches should be tackled in low gears and sitting on the saddle. Those who choose the rocking position, are concentrating on strength endurance. This should not really play a dominant role in the first week of training. Uphill phases concentrating more on strength endurance should be kept for the second part of the training block.

Due to metabolic processes in the body, the third day of such a training holiday - normally involving a significant change of climate - should always be an active rest day. Very gentle pedalling for 1-2 hours is advisable here.

I must warn against letting every calmly planned training ride turn into a race, often leading to total exhaustion. After 6-7 days at the latest, an athlete is irrevocably burnt out. It's often not possible to do training every day in the second week as the first injuries have set in. The remaining days are then just wasted. The body then gets its rest phases through injuries and colds.

What form can such a cycling block take? Here is a concrete example from my own experience:

The training obective at all times must be: even on the last day at training camp, one should still be capable of doing normal training. In other words 'build-up' and not 'break-down' training is on the agenda. My seasonal goal here was participation in an

Ironman triathlon. The important parameters are morning pulse at rest and the training feeling. If one's pulse at rest is 7-8 beats higher per minute, only a short and particularly relaxed cycling session or even a break from training should follow.

Starting out in mid-April: 450 miles cycling completed and weekly running sessions of between 20 and 30 miles.

Pulse at rest: 47-48

Day	Cycling completed in miles	Intensity	Further Training
1	56	calm	
2	72	relaxed	7 miles run
3	30	very calm	regeneration
4	78	relaxed	
5	-		8 miles run
6	62	hilly area	1km swim in the sea
7	97	calm, sometimes mountainous	
8	-		8 miles run
9	78	with brisk sections	
10	60	mountainous	
11	-		1km swim, 8 miles run
12	44	relaxed	8 miles run, fast
13	84	very mountainous	
14			8 miles run

In other words I cycled a total of 660 miles, ran 47 miles and swam 2km within 14 days. Average cycling speed was 16mph. heart rates during cycling training were between 120-125 on average.

What followed this was a genuine week of regeneration with several bike rides to work and two runs of 8 and 9 miles.

Some Points of Advice for Cycling Training

▲ Always cycle with a helmet.

▲ Have spare tubes and a mini-repair set with you.

▲ Mount a number of bottle-holders onto the bike.

▲ Ensure an optimal rpm of 100-110 per minute.

▲ Have sufficient liquid and food with you on longer training routes.

▲ Always have something to eat with you to prevent hunger setting in.

▲ Change gears early enough when cycling uphill.

▲ In the first weeks of the preparation period, only cycle with the small chain gear.

▲ Sunglasses protect you from sun, insects and wind.

▲ Increase volume first and then intensity.

▲ It is possible to carry out endurance training after strength training in one day - but not the other way around.

▲ Stick to your regeneration weeks.

▲ When doing interval training it is important to do 15-20 minutes of both warm-up and cool-down cycling.

▲ Gradually accustom yourself to the desired speed.

▲ Begin with short route sections.

▲ Intervals should be directed towards one's seasonal aim.

▲ Have variety in the intervals, change load duration and load intensity frequently.

▲ Carry out interval training regularly, but at most only once a week over a period of four weeks, then go two weeks without it and begin again for a maximum of four weeks. Alternative rhythm: 1x intervals once a week for two weeks, one week without, and then another two weeks of interval training.

▲ Make sure that the breaks between intervals are long enough, keep on pedalling easily until pulse falls to under 110 beats per minute.

▲ When a bike is transported by air, never have air pressure cartridges with it!

▲ Training alternatives with unfavorable weather conditions: mountain bike, training on the roll, spinning.

Cycling in Competition

During competition there are a number of particular aspects which I have summarized briefly here.

▲ Never rub in sun cream on your forehead, as sweat dissolves even waterproof cream and this can cause very unpleasant burning in the eyes.
▲ Road Traffic Regulations are valid here, therefore never cycle over the middle line.

▲ Help from others is not allowed.

▲ On the day before the competition, cover the cycling distance either with the car or v-e-r-y s-l-o-w-l-y on the bike.

▲ Shake some talcum powder inside your cycling shoes if not wearing socks.

▲ In extreme heat do not pump up tires higher than 8 bar/ 116 lbs/sq.in.

▲ Attach start numbers to a rubber band.

▲ Wear shoes with velcro fastening.

▲ Wear sunglasses to protect yourself from the sunshine and the flies.

▲ Have your bike ready in the right gear and with a full drink bottle.

▲ Begin with a high pedalling frequency.

▲ Begin taking in liquids early enough.

▲ Eat solid foods in small chunks.

▲ Never cycle *dry*, accept drinks early enough.

▲ Optimum rpm in competition: 90

▲ Change gears in time when riding uphill, never drag yourself up the hill.

▲ Wear close-fitting cycling clothing.

▲ In cool, damp weather have a thin raincoat with you just in case.

▲ Ride the last few minutes with somewhat less pressure to loosen up your muscles for running.

▲ Only unstrap and take off your helmet in the transition zone. Undoing the chin strap too soon can lead to disqualification.

The Heart Rate Phases during Cycling Training

In the training suggestions that follow, I would like to deal with specific training intensities for cycling sessions as well. The following table shows the relevant intensities, expressed as a proportion of maximum pulse in percentage terms in each case.

Step	Description of Training	Cycling Training as % of Maximum Heart rate	Form of Training	Cycling Training - My maximum pulse	Comparison with Running Training % of Max. Heart rate
1	Easy-going, refreshing Regeneration	55-65	Fat Burning - Basic Endurance		60-70
2	Calm Training	65-70	Basic Endurance		70-75
3	Easy Training	70	Basic Endurance		75
4	Brisk Training	70-75	Endurance Training		75-80
5	Very Brisk Training (fast)	75-80	Speed Endurance Training		80-85
6	Hard Training	80-85	Tempo Ride		85-90

The heart rates for cycling are 5% lower than those for running training in each heart rate phase.

CHAPTER 6

Swimming

The Most Difficult Discipline For Masters!

Of all three disciplines, swimming is by far the most difficult for the majority of Masters, except of course if your name is Kalli NOTTRODT, a swimmer before becoming a triathlete. "You can't teach an old dog new tricks," is true for many Masters. From the aspect of implementing it accurately, swimming is more complicated than running and cycling, and also requires more intensive training. As well as this, one has to build up one's good form in a swimming pool and then have to try and use these skills effectively in open waters with 1 800 other participants!

There are a few tricks, however, which make it possible to prepare oneself optimally for swimming in a lake or in the sea.

As can be seen in the table in Chapter 5, swimming takes up 10-14% of the Middle and Ironman Distances from a time aspect. Nevertheless, swimming is of great importance. Any athlete who doesn't keep a cool head in open water with 1 800 other starters, might not 'sink' but will definitely lose a significant amount of time. Time, which he simply doesn't have later for a good placement, for the qualification, for whatever.

Swimming training works on coordination, speed, strength endurance, involves a lot of muscle work while being kind to ligaments and joints. Regular swimming training improves the condition of the muscles of the upper body, which in turn reaps visual benfits for cycling. Since the breaststroke puts strain on the neck muscles and the knees, both of which are under strong demand during the other two disciplines of cycling and running, one can recommend using the quicker crawl stroke.

The most important points about swimming, such as
▲ swimming equipment
▲ adjustment from breast stroke to the crawl
▲ basic crawling technique
▲ most common errors with the crawl stroke

have already been looked at in great detail in "Lifelong Success - Triathlon: Training for Masters." So as to avoid repeating myself I would like to deal with swimming training for the keen and ambitious Masters in this book, various swimming schedules and swimming in open waters.

Swimming Training

The main differences between swimming training for Masters who are preparing for the Middle and Ironman distances and the necessary training for the shorter distances, can be seen in the longer intervals and the more frequent inclusion of continuous swims. Swimming is the one discipline where one can change training content from one session to the next. One should make frequent use of this chance to avoid falling into a rut of monotonous rhythm e.g with 4 x 500yds, 2 x 1,000yds. An athlete who wishes to improve his swimming performance should head for the pool 2-3 times a week. During the direct preparation for the triathlon season one should also practice training in a neoprene suit. Open waters are more suitable for this than a swimming pool.

During the swimming month, one should try and get out swimming 3-4 times a week to create a solid base for the entire season. The following list of 14 different training workouts shows which training components one can work with. These can be supplemented or simply practiced more often in training.

Each session of swimming training should consist of five steps:
▲ Stretching exercises
▲ Warm-up swimming
▲ **Swimming workout**
▲ Cool-down swimming
▲ Stretching exercises

The stretching exercises before training, i.e. in a cold state, should be carried out a little more cautiously than those after training. (Exercises, see Lifelong Success - Triathlon: Training for Masters). Warm-up swimming over 200-400yds should be playful with several short sprints.

Cool-down swimming over 100-200yds is done with whichever stroke is desired, and ends each training session.

14 swimming workouts are listed below from which you can set up your own individual program. All workouts can be easily altered, adjusted, supplemented and condensed.

The 14 Swimming Workouts for Pools and Open Water

Nr.	Swimming workout	Total Distance in yds
1	* 400yds warm-up swimming as desired, change strokes * 4 x 500yds crawl, five-, four-, three-, two-stroke * Easy tempo, accurate technique * 100yds calm each time in between * Cool-down swimming, 200yds breast	2,900
2	* Warm-up swimming, 200yds breaststroke calm, 200yds as desired * 100yds crawl, touch off * 200yds crawl, five-stroke * 300yds, 100yds right stroke only, 100yds left stroke only, 100yds normal * 400yds, 50yds only legs + 150yds complete position, and repeat * 300yds, tempo increases before and after the turn. * 200yds, crawl, three-stroke * 100yds, sprint * 4 x 50yds, 25yds relaxed, 25yds fast, 1 min. break * Cool-down swim, 200yds as desired	2,400

3	* Warm-up Swim, 200yds as desired	2,600
	* 2 x 1,000yds crawl, relaxed, conscious breathing	
	* Cool-down swim, 400yds crawl and - technique exercises	

3
* Warm-up Swim, 200yds as desired   2,600
* 2 x 1,000yds crawl, relaxed, conscious breathing
* Cool-down swim, 400yds crawl and - technique exercises

4
* Warm-up swim, 400yds as desired   3,200
* 10x 200yds, crawl, break 45 seconds
* 100yds calm - with rounded fist
* 5 x 100yds crawl, after each 100yds speed up a little
* Cool-down swim, 200yds breast

5
* Warm-up swim, 200yds breast   3,100
* 6x 200yds crawl and breast alternately, break 45 seconds
* Breast calm, crawl fast
* 200yds calm
* 3x 150yds crawl, every 50yds five-, four-, three- stroke
* 50yds calm
* 800yds crawl, pay particular attention to good technique!
* Cool-down swim, 200yds breast

6
* Warm-up swim, 400yds as desired   2,700
* 800yds crawl, three-stroke
* 400yds crawl, 100yds right arm only, 100yds left arm only, 100yds touch-off, 100yds normal
* 200yds, crawl legs only
* 200yds, crawl arms only
* 8x 50yds crawl legs, break 40 seconds
* Cool-down swim, 400yds calm

7 * Warm-up swim, 200yds breast,   2,600
    200yds crawl, 200yds backstroke
   * 10 x 100yds crawl, break 30 seconds
   * 500yds crawl with speed-ups
   * Cool-down swim, 500yds all strokes

8 * Warm-up swim, 400yds relaxed   1,900
    with technique exercises, e.g. fist,
    high elbow etc
   * 10 x 150yds crawl in 1 000yds-
    competition-tempo
   * Cool-down swim, 200yds backstroke

9 * Warm-up swim, 200yds breast,   2,900
    200yds back
   * 1,000yds with breathing exercises,
    2 minutes above best time
   * Break 2 minutes
   * 1,000yds with technique exercises,
    2 minutes above best time
   * Cool-down swim, 500yds all strokes

10 * Warm-up swim, 400yds crawl   2,900
   * 6x 200yds crawl (legs,arms, total
    position)
   * 200yds breast
   * 5x 100yds crawl, fast, tempo,
    1min. break each time
   * 200yds breast relaxed,
   * 4x 50yds crawl, 25yds relaxed,
    25yds sprint, break 30 seconds
   * Cool-down swim, 200yds as de-
    sired

11	* Warm-up swim, 200yds as desired	2,200
	* Pyramid swimming, crawl	
	* 50yds/100yds/150yds/200yds/250yds/ 250yds/200yds/150yds/100yds/ 50yds alternately relaxed and brisk, break 20-30 seconds each time	
	* 200yds breast	
	* Cool-down swim, 300yds all strokes	
12	* Warm-up swim, 300yds as desired	2,600
	* 100yds/200yds/300yds/400yds/ 400yds/ 300yds/200yds/100yds	
	* First half relaxed, other half brisk each time	
	* Cool-down swimming, 300yds as desired	
13	* Swimming in open waters	3,000-5,000
	* approx. 10 min warm-up swim	
	* Use width, length of lake or distance up to buoy as interval distance	
	* Indicated distance, alternately relaxed and brisk	
	* Alternative: 100 breaths relaxed, 50 breaths fast,	
	* 200 breaths relaxed, 100 fast	
14	* Swimming in Open Waters	3,000-5,000
	* Continuous method: Warm-up swim, 30 or 60 minutes Continuous Swim, Cool-down swim	
	* Alternative: 30 min fast, 30 min relaxed	

* Fartlek in water with or without neoprene suit
* Practice swimming start with 200yds sprint followed by 500yds normal swimming speed
* Practice climbing out of the water: swim until it is possible to touch the ground with your hands

In order to improve strength endurance while swimming, one can recommend the occasional use of paddles. With the pullbuoy pressed between the thighs, one is also better able to check arm-strokes. Particularly helpful here are swimming goggles, which enable a viewing spectrum of 180°.

The swimming section for the Middle and Ironman distances generally takes place in open waters. There are a number of important aspects to be considered here compared with swimming in a pool.

Swimming in Open Water: How Do I Prepare Myself for this?

There are a number of important differences between swimming in open waters and swimming in a pool.

As the long swimming distances generally take place in open water, it is advisable to prepare oneself for this early enough. Compared with swimming in a swimming pool, with its deep blue water, the differences are as follows:

▲ Murky waters
▲ Orientation not possible underwater, orientation is only possible over the surface

▲ Lower temperatures than in a swimming pool
▲ Changeable current conditions and wave influences
▲ Sometimes saltwater
▲ Mass start with more than 1,000 participants
▲ Swimming in a neoprene suit.
▲ Exit onto the beach.

The only positive factor, when compared with swimming in a pool, is the neoprene suit. Due to the improved position in the water, one is also capable of achieving better swimming times. The weaker swimmers among us profit considerably from this. It can happen that one's swimming time with a neoprene suit is 2 min faster per kilometer than without. However one must be prepared for its tight fit early enough as well its impedance on the stroke and leg movement. Neoprene suits are not permitted in Hawaii due to the high water temperatures.

Despite all this there are only marginal differences between the two swimming competitions as far as swimming technique is concerned. Included here is the lower amount of leg work on the long swimming distances and the fact that one must adapt one's breathing and rhythm to fit in with the frequently changing conditions.

The lower amount of leg work during the swimming section of a triathlon can firstly be explained by the fact that the legs have to face much more strain in both of the endurance disciplines that follow, and secondly, the fact that the use of a neoprene suit improves one's position in the water.

Athletes who almost exclusively train in a swimming pool must prepare themselves mentally for these major differences beforehand and, as well as this, they should try and go swimming in open waters more often in the summer months, in order to be able to get partially accustomed at least to the several unforeseeable factors.

Some Points of Advice for Swimming Competitions in Open Waters

▲ Check out the starting area well before the start.

▲ Make sure you're familiar with the exact route of the swimming distance. What buoys do I have to swim round and how?

▲ Do a warm-up swim 10 minutes before the start.

▲ Locate orientation aids plenty of time in advance (buoys, building, towers, trees in the background etc).

▲ Give yourself a realistic starting placement.

▲ Try as quickly as possible to achieve a good swimming position, a position in which you are able to swim relatively unhindered. I personally am prepared to swim a bit longer for this.

▲ Try and find your own swimming rhythm as quickly as possible.

▲ Do not swim at other athletes' shoulder level, as the water stirred up here can easily get into your mouth during the breathing phase. It's better to swim at the other athlete's hip level. This supports optimum gliding in the water.

▲ Aim for your own orientation markings. Don't just rely on the people ahead of you.

▲ After every 5-10 two- or three-phase breathing strokes, orientate yourself by briefly turning your head around to the front.

▲ Concentrate on your own technique.

▲ Don't shoot your bolt in the first discipline, there are two long and exerting distances to follow.

▲ Swim the last 200yds calmly and prepare yourself for the first transition.

▲ Do not get up out of the water until you can touch the ground with your hands.

▲ Be careful about rubbing sun cream onto your forehead before competition. Firstly your swimming goggles are quite likely to slip out of place because of the cream, particularly when one wears the big goggles with the 180° viewing.

Secondly, this waterproof layer of cream can suddenly dissolve during the cycling section due to profuse sweating; this causes such an extreme irritation of the eyes that it is necessary to get off your bike a number of times and rinse out your eyes thoroughly.

CHAPTER 7

Combination Training

Transition: Cycle/Run

Combination training, i.e. carrying out two disciplines immediately after each other, should be practiced regularly both before and during the competition period. The first transition in triathlon from swimming to cycling is first and foremost an organizational transition. It doesn't pose many problems for the muscles, as leg work while swimming is reduced to a minimum due to the long distances and the wearing of neoprene suits in particular.

The second combination in triathlon - cycling to running - is tricky by comparison. Anyone who doesn't practice this transition regularly, starts off running with an unfamiliar feeling of 'lead' in his legs and thus doesn't reach his usual running rhythm until much later. Time losses are the inevitable consequence.

It's a good idea to cut down one's pressure on the pedals for the last two cycling miles and loosen up the muscles a bit by cycling at a higher rpm.

When doing combination training for the long triathlon distances, one can practice the transitions in three different forms:

▲ Long, relaxed endurance bike ride followed directly by a fast, short run.
e.g. 60 miles cycle, relaxed + 5 miles run, quick.

▲ Short, quick training session on the bike followed directly by a long, calm run.
e.g. 35-40 miles cycle, quick + 12 mile run, calm

▲ Quick run (warm-up beforehand), followed directly by a short, brisk cycle.
e.g. 5 mile run, quick + 20 miles, brisk.

An athlete who practices this situation regularly has clear advantages during this second transition; a transition which is difficult for all triathletes.

The first transition from swimming to cycling is mainly an organizational transition. The important thing here is to possess all the necessary equipment, have it in good condition and then place them in the right order in the transition zone. One should also remember that it's better to have an extra jacket ready than to be shivering the whole time during the cycle.

CHAPTER 8

Training for the Middle Distance

In Chapter 2 I already pointed out that one cannot take on the Middle distance with its 1.2/56/13 miles, i.e. 70.2 miles in total, without proper preparation. The requirements necessary in order to successfully complete this interesting and challenging distance were also explained. Now we want to look at training in concrete terms.

The training plans that follow show one possibility for organizing one's training successfully.

Good to very good basic endurance is the basis for training for the Middle distance. Newcomers in the Middle distance are not new to triathlon, they are athletes who wish to 'move up' from the Short triathlon distance to the next one, the Middle triathlon (category). The 'Ironman' goal gets nearer and nearer for many athletes now, and their motivation then rises too.

Before taking part in one's first Middle triathlon, which is not on the agenda until the end of June, one should plan at least one short triathlon. This can be part of one's training schedule. At the same time, however, it offers an athlete the opportunity to test his form and his equipment. One can take part in a second Middle triathlon in August or at the beginning of September as a finish-off to the season.

In between there's plenty of room for a few Short distance competitions.

Regular winter training with the emphasis on running and swimming is what is neccessary for a triathlon program like this. From January onwards one should do swimming training 1-2 x a week as well as some calm continuous runs. Former runners

might plan a spring marathon for March or April. This is followed up with a regeneration phase of three weeks, consisting of relaxed swimming and cycling training in particular, before starting proper training of all three disciplines.

Without including the marathon mentioned and without emphasising one particular sport, **weekly** training could be as follows:

January:
* 1-2 x swimming (schedule examples, Chapter 6)
* Running, 1 x 12-16 miles at the weekend, calm
* 1 x 9 miles fartlek, 1 x 8 miles relaxed, stretching exercises

February:
* 2 x swimming, first cycling trips, maybe the roller device.
* 2 x running, 1 x 2 hours calm, 1 x 1:15 hours with fartlek

March:
* 2 x swimming
* 3 x running, 1 x 12-16 miles calm, 1 x 1:15 hours relaxed, 1 x 10km continuous tempo run with 80-85% intensity, or participation in 6-9 mile fun-runs every two weeks, stretching exercises
* Use the weekends for cycling

April:
* Cycling emphasis on bank holidays and weekends 25, 35 and 50 miles or even 60 miles calm cycling trips, easy pedalling, 3 x cycling a week in total.
* 1-2 x swimming, intervals 3 x 500yds; 10 x 100yds, 5 x 200yds, pyramid
* 2 x running, 1 x 12-16 miles calm, 1 x fartlek 10 miles

May:
* 2 x swimming, 2 x running, 2 x cycling, stretching exercises
* For the last six weeks running up to one's first middle triathlon have a look at the following weekly plans

Middle Triathlon Training with the Aim to "Finish"

Training Emphasis: Cycling + Swimming   week: 1

Date: from _____ until _____

Day	Weight lbs (a.m.)	S Dist. yds	S Time	C Dist. mi	C Time	R Dist. mi	R Time	Other sporting activity	Comment	Pulse Rest/Strain	Weight (p.m.)
Mon.				25	relaxed						
Tues.		1.000	Interv.								
Wed.				50	brisk						
Thur.						9	calm	stretching*			
Fri.											
Sat.				30	relaxed	12	brisk	*	Combin. Training C + R		
Sun.		2,000	Endur.		calm						
Total:		3,000		105		21					

Training Emphasis: Running, Half-distance Marathon of 21 km

Date: from   until   week: 2

Day	Weight lbs (a.m.)	S Dist. yds	S Time	C Dist. mi	C Time	R Dist. mi	R Time	Other sporting activity	Comment	Pulse Rest/Strain	Weight (p.m.)
Mon.											
Tues.		1,500	Interv.	35	FL	11	calm	*			
Wed.						9	relaxed	*			
Thur.				45	calm						
Fri.											
Sat.						13		*	Half-distance marathon competition		
Sun.		2,000	Endur.								
Total:		3,500		80		33					

Training Emphasis: Regeneration

Date: from _____ until _____   week: 3

Day	Weight lbs (a.m.)	S Dist. yds	Time	C Dist. mi	Time	R Dist. mi	Time	Other sporting activity	Comment	Pulse Rest/Strain	Weight (p.m.)
Mon.											
Tues.		2,000				5	Regen.	*	S: 3x500yds Endurance		
Wed.				30	calm						
Thur.						9	relaxed	*			
Fri.											
Sat.				30	brisk	8	calm	*	Combin. Training C + R		
Sun.		2,000	relaxed								
Total:		4,000		60		22					

Training Emphasis: Cycling

Date: from   until   week: 4

Day	Weight lbs (a.m.)	S Dist. yds	S Time	C Dist. mi	C Time	R Dist. mi	R Time	Other sporting activity	Comment	Pulse Rest/Strain	Weight (p.m.)
Mon.				25	quick			*	C: 3x5 mi quick		
Tues.		1,500				9	FL				
Wed.				35	relaxed						
Thur.						16	slow	*	3x Long, continuous run		
Fri.											
Sat.				70	brisk	3	calm	*	Cycling Tour		
									C + short R		
Sun.		2,000	2x1,000								
Total:		3,500		130		28					

Training Emphasis: Swimming, Cycling, Running

Date: from   until   week: 5

Day	Weight lbs (a.m.)	S		C		R		Other sporting activity	Comment	Pulse Rest/ Strain	Weight (p.m.)
		Dist. yds	Time	Dist. mi	Time	Dist. mi	Time				
Mon.		1,500	Endur.	25	1 hour tempo			*			
Tues.						9	FL	*			
Wed.				35	relaxed						
Thur.						16	slow	*	3x Long, continuous run		
Fri.											
Sat.				50	brisk	5	calm	*	Combin. Training C + R		
Sun.		2,500	Interv.								
Total:		4,000		110		30					

Training Emphasis: Middle distance

Date: from _____ until _____   week: 6

Day	Weight lbs (a.m.)	S Dist. yds	S Time	C Dist. mi	C Time	R Dist. mi	R Time	Other sporting activity	Comment	Pulse Rest/Strain	Weight (p.m.)
Mon.				30	FL			*			
Tues.		1,200	relaxed			9	short FL	*			
Wed.											
Thur.				20	calm						
Fri.											
Sat.		2,000		56		13		*	Middle Triathlon		
Sun.				20	calm, regen.						
Total:		1,200 + 2,000		70 + 56		9 + 13					

An athlete who trains for his first Middle triathlon in a similar way to above, can feel confident going to the start. Obviously with this relatively low amount of time invested, one cannot expect to be right up among the leaders, but it should be definitely fun. The target one sets is to finish and not to win.

Those wishing to devote more time to training (e.g. Masters who have now retired from work) are welcome to do so. However, they should particularly heed the general training principles (Chapter 10): regeneration weeks, training within a group, generally selecting a training speed at which one is able to hold a conversation, etc.

In the last week before a Middle triathlon one should carry out so little training that one heads to the start with a guilty conscience. A few relaxed training sessions ought to be on the agenda however.

Chapter 11 describes in great detail the very last competition preparations as well as the day of competition itself.

The transition phase must not be as hectic as in the short or sprinting distance. In cold weather it is not just a good idea to dry oneself down and take a change of clothes after the swimming discipline, it's **vital**. What are 60 seconds compared with possible health risks such as kidney problems among others?

Training Plans for Competitive Masters

An athlete who wants more than just to finish on the Middle distance, has gathered a lot of experience in the field of triathlon. The majority of Masters belong to this category. Mostly they have the advantage that they have been carrying out their sporting activities for many years and therefore have good to very good basic endurance.

An athlete who wishes to take a more 'competitive' part in the Middle distance, should try to achieve the following individual performances:

2 000yds swimming < 42 minutes
25 miles cycling < 1:12 hours
10km run < 42 minutes

It is possible to build oneself up using this as a basis.

More detailed information on swimming, cycling or running can be found in the relevant chapters. In the following training program I have assumed that the main competition takes place in June. They can be moved around to comply with those regions where the competitions take place at an earlier or later stage.

Possible Year Structure

Transitional Period: October, November, December and perhaps January. 2x a week relaxed trot in 1-1:15 hours, a light cycling trip if possible, 1-2 x a week relaxed swimming with technique exercises. Analysis of previous season, planning of new season.

Preparation Period 1 and 11: February, March, April, May.

Competition Period: End of May- September

January:

First part of the preparation period. Training volume increases at a low level of physical intensity, heart rates 130. Make use of cross-country skiing opportunities. Stretching exercises and light strength exercises support all-round blood circulation in the body.

Running, approx. 30-35 miles, steady continuous runs, 1x a week long, continuous run of 16 miles. An athlete wishing to run his spring marathon, runs for 18 miles. Occasional participation in popular runs, however not with maximum effort. In dry weather, 1 hour cycling trip at the weekend. Athletes who enjoy cycling on the 'roller' may prepare for cycling training in this way.

Swimming: 2-3 x a week, technique training, endurance swimming and intervals.

February: Swimming Month

The motto here is to swim as often as possible. An athlete living near a swimming pool, or who can avail of such an opportunity in his lunch break, will obviously do more swimming than someone who has to drive 12 miles to get there in the first place. Ideal would be 4x a week, 2,000-2,500yds each week. For more details on swimming training, see swimming workout in Chapter 6.

Running: Per week 1x 8 miles, 9 miles fartlek, 12 miles calm.

Cycling: Depending on weather relaxed cycling trips with 100 rpm.

March: Running Month

As well as the normal swimming training, 2-3 x per week running, 1 x endurance and 2 x intervals. Cycling trips are on the agenda at the weekend and 1x a week, so as to prepare for the cycling month in April. Cycling to work would be ideal.

The emphasis is on running in this month. It's just as possible to have January: swimming month, February: running month, March: cycling month and mid-late April for the spring marathon.

One ought to have 3-4 running sessions a week, 1x long 16 miles, one brisk run + two relaxed runs. Detailed instructions for marathon runs can be found in Chapter 4. Important here : don't forget stretching exercises for those parts of the body which were under particular strain.

April: Cycling Month

Athletes who have completed their spring marathon, can, apart from the relaxed runs in this regeneration phase, devote a lot more time to swimming and cycling. Emphasis cycling takes place on the weekends and over the Easter Holidays. Tours of up to 60 miles with 100-110 r.p.m on the small chain gear are important here. e.g. Fridays, 45 miles, Saturdays 60 miles + 5 mile run, Sundays 56 miles, Wednesdays 30 miles. The main priority here is basic endurance in cycling, and for this reason it only makes sense to start with intervals at the end of this month at the earliest. Place name sign tests bring variety into this month.

A two-week training holiday in sunny regions would obviously be ideal here. There is not only enough time for training here but also plenty of time for private activities. 700 miles in two weeks is a good base for the oncoming season.

Running 2-3 x 1:00-1:15 hours.

May:

At the weekends, practice the cycle-run transition. In each case one session relaxed, the other brisk. 1x a week a quick cycling session e.g. in/out 3 x 2 mile interval, the same distance with easy pedalling in between; 3 x 3 miles, 3 miles relaxed in between.

Week Rhythm: N:N:R (normal/normal/ regeneration).

Swimming as in April, intervals, 1 x continuous swim.

Running: 1 x per week intervals: in/out 2 x 5,000yds at 85%, 6-8 x 1,000yds at 10km running speed, trotting break 1 km until pulse reaches 110.

Short triathlon competition as a 'dress rehearsal'.

June: see training plans.

July: After the Middle Triathlon come two weeks of regenerative training (R), after that normal (N), i.e. R:R:N. Further Short and Middle triathlons are possible in the months of August and September.

Triathlon training in June for the Middle distance could take the following form:

Note: This 'sample plan' cannot take your own circumstances into consideration, but rather give a general outline of how you could organize your training. You have to adjust this plan to fit in with with your personal situation.

Competition Preparation directly before the competition, and **the day of the competition** itself is looked at and explained in great detail in Chapter 11 regarding the Ironman competition.

Four-week Training Plan for the Middle Distance

Training Emphasis: Cycling Emphasis Training, Combination Training
Previous Week and First Part of Week Regeneration

Date: from   until   week:

Day	Weight lbs (a.m.)	S Dist. yds	S Time	C Dist. mi	C Time	R Dist. mi	R Time	Other sporting activity	Comment	Pulse Rest/Strain	Weight (p.m.)
Mon.											
Tues.		2,000	Interv.			8	relaxed	Stretching			
Wed.				60	calm			*			
Thur.				50	brisk			*			
Fri.											
Sat.				45	brisk	8	relaxed	*	Combin. Training C + R		
Sun.		2,500	Endur.			9	with FL	*			
Total:		4,500		155		25					

Training Emphasis: Swimming, Cycling, Running, Combination Training

Date: from ___ until ___ week:

Day	Weight lbs (a.m.)	S Dist. yds	S Time	C Dist. mi	C Time	R Dist. mi	R Time	Other sporting activity	Comment	Pulse Rest/Strain	Weight (p.m.)
Mon.											
Tues.		2,500	Interv.			9	Quick	*	R: 2x3 miles		
Wed.				60	calm			*			
Thur.		2,000	Interv.	30	4x5 quick			*	C: 4x3 miles		
Fri.						15	calm	*			
Sat.		2,000	Endur.	56	brisk	3	relaxed	*	Combin. Training C + R		
Sun.		2,500	Endur.			9	calm	*	S + R		
Total:		9,000		146		36					

Training Emphasis: Penultimate Week with the Last Long Running and Cycling Sessions

Date: from   until   week:

Day	Weight lbs (a.m.)	S Dist. yds	S Time	C Dist. mi	C Time	R Dist. mi	R Time	Other sporting activity	Comment	Pulse Rest/ Strain	Weight (p.m.)
Mon.											
Tues.		2,000				9	Quick sections	*	R: 6x 1,000 m TT		
Wed.				70	relaxed			*			
Thur.		2,000									
Fri.				35	Quick sections	16	calm	*	C: 3x6 miles quick		
Sat.				50	calm	8	relaxed	*			
Sun.		3,000	Endur.								
Total:		7,000		155		33					

Training Emphasis: Middle Triathlon Competition, Regeneration beforehand

Date: from ____ until ____ week: ____

Day	Weight lbs (a.m.)	S Dist. yds	S Time	C Dist. mi	C Time	R Dist. mi	R Time	Other sporting activity	Comment	Pulse Rest/ Strain	Weight (p.m.)
Mon.									Regen.		
Tues.				30		8	calm	*	C: 12 miles 85%		
Wed.						6		*	R: 2.5 miles, 90%		
Thur.		2,000	relaxed	25	relaxed						
Fri.		1,000	Endur.								
Sat.						3	Trot	*			
Sun.		2,200		56		13		*	Middle Triathlon		
Total:		3,000 + 2,200		55 + 56		17 + 13					

TT = 10km tempo

As an alternative I would also like to illustrate a six-week plan stemming from triathlon practical experience. The athlete's strong and weak points as well as his personal circumstances have an influence on this plan.

Training for the Middle Distance, the last six weeks

Master athlete, 53 years old, 17th triathlon season, training investment: 380 hours/year.

April: Two weeks of cycling block training with 750 miles cycling, 37 miles running, and 2km swimming.

A few words of explanation on this plan:

2 x 8 miles cycling represent the cycling distance to and from work. The original plan for the week (two days load, one day rest, three days load, one day rest) could not be kept up in practice. This was due to familiar factors such as: career, family, weather conditions, leisure and many more.

Because of the short competitions - sprint triathlon and duathlon - normal training was able to be calmer than it would have been without competitions.

Emphasis: Regeneration

Date: from 1.5   until 7.5   week: 1 Middle Triathlon

Day	Weight lbs (a.m.)	S Dist. yds	S Time	C Dist. mi	C Time	R Dist. mi	R Time	Other sporting activity	Comment	Pulse Rest/Strain	Weight (p.m.)
Mon.											
Tues.										46	
Wed.				8 + 8		9	1:13h	stretching	Pulse 127		
Thur.				8 + 8				*			
Fri.				16	calm	8	relaxed	*			
Sat.											
Sun.		500	10:10	12		3		1:08:50h *	Sprint Triathlon		
Total:		500		60		20					

Emphasis: Swimming in Open Water + Running

Date: from 8.5   until 14.5   week: 2 Middle Triathlon

Day	Weight lbs (a.m.)	S Dist. yds	S Time	C Dist. mi	C Time	R Dist. mi	R Time	Other sporting activity	Comment	Pulse Rest/ Strain	Weight (p.m.)
Mon.		1,800		8 + 8		8	1:00	*			
Tues.											
Wed.				8 + 8		9	1:08 FL	*			176
Thur.	172.5			8 70	17.2mph			*			
Fri.		2,000	Lake			11	1:20	*	Running Pulse 130		
Sat.		3,000	Lake							48	
Sun.		4,000	Lake			10	1:25				
Total:		10,800		110		38					

Emphasis: Duathlon Competition

Date: from 15.5   until 21.5   week: 3 Middle Triathlon

Day	Weight lbs (a.m.)	S Dist. yds	S Time	C Dist. mi	C Time	R Dist. mi	R Time	Other sporting activity	Comment	Pulse Rest/Strain	Weight (p.m.)
Mon.				8+8		8	calm	*			
Tues.				8+8							
Wed.						9	1:12	*	Pulse 130		
Thur.				8+30							
Fri.				25	very calm				Relaxing Cycle Tour		
Sat.											
Sun.		6mi	run	26	cycling	3	run	*	Duathlon 2:26h		
Total:		6		121		20					

Emphasis: Cycling + Running, Sprint Triathlon

Date: from 22.5   until 28.5   week: 4 Middle Triathlon

Day	Weight lbs (a.m.)	S Dist. yds	S Time	C Dist. mi	C Time	R Dist. mi	R Time	Other sporting activity	Comment	Pulse Rest/Strain	Weight (p.m.)
Mon.		1,800	3×500	8 + 8		8	0:59	*	Dog tired in the evening		
Tues.										53	
Wed.				8 + 8		17	2:15	*	Relaxed run		
Thur.				8 + 8		6			Accompanied on bike by grandchild		
Fri.				95	17.1mph	6		*	Combin. Training C + R calm		
Sat.										46	
Sun.		500	10:04	13	22.4mph	3	Run	1:08h	Sprint-TRI		
Total:		2,300		156		40					

Emphasis: Middle Triathlon

Date: from 29.5   until 4.6   week: 5 Middle Triathlon

Day	Weight lbs (a.m.)	S Dist. yds	S Time	C Dist. mi	C Time	R Dist. mi	R Time	Other sporting activity	Comment	Pulse Rest/Strain	Weight (p.m.)
Mon.		2,000	3x500			8	0:58	*			
Tues.				8 + 8							
Wed.				8 + 8		9	1:06	*	Running Pulse, brisk	141	177.5
Thur.	174			45	13mph				C very calm		
Fri.						8	1:05				
Sat.				20					C relaxed		
Sun.		2,000	0:43	54	2:36	13	1:25	4:44:52h great	Middle Triathlon		
Total:		2,000 + 2,000		97 + 54		25 + 13					

Emphasis: Regeneration Week, Swimming in Lake, Ironman Preparation

Date: from 5.6   until 11.6   week: 6 Middle Triathlon

Day	Weight lbs (a.m.)	S Dist. yds	S Time	C Dist. mi	C Time	R Dist. mi	R Time	Other sporting activity	Comment	Pulse Rest/ Strain	Weight (p.m.)
Mon.		1,800	relaxed						Tired		
Tues.				8 + 8					Tired		
Wed.				8 + 8		9	1:20	*	Calm run		
Thur.											
Fri.		2,500	Lake			8			Running still hard		
Sat.		2,500	Lake	62	15.5mph						
Sun.											
Total:		6,800		94		17					

A Master who wishes to compare his competition times with those of a top-class athlete may do this using the table below. Using the age coefficients according to CEPELKA one comes up with interesting results.

Age	Age coefficient	**4:00h**	4:20h	4:40h	5:00h	**5:20h**
27,28	1.0000	4:00	4:20	4:40	5:00	5:20
30	0.9927	4:02	4:22	4:42	5:02	5:12
35	0.9690	4:08	4:28	4:49	5:10	5:30
40	0.9410	4:15	4:36	**4:58**	5:19	5:40
45	0.9132	4:23	4:44	5:07	5:29	5:50
50	0.8854	4:31	4:54	5:16	5:39	6:00
55	0.8575	4:40	5:04	5:27	5:50	6:12
60	0.8252	4:51	5:16	5:39	6:04	6:28
65	0.7817	5:07	5:32	5:58	6:24	**6:48**
70	0.7253	5:30	5:58	6:26	6:53	7:20

Triathlon Performances on the Middle Distance according to age

According to this table a time of 4:40h by a 55-year-old athlete is comparable with 4:00h by a top-class athlete.

This calculation is interesting, but should not be the decisive factor for a Master's sporting activity. Women even achieve a 10% bonus here, due to their lower muscle proportion. Thus a finishing time of 5:00h by a woman is comparable with a man's finishing time of 4:30h, without taking age coefficient into consideration.

CHAPTER 9

Training for the Ironman Distance

Which triathlete doesn't dream of finishing in an Ironman and thus becoming a member of the 'triathlon aristocracy'. A further dream for many is then culminated with the Ironman in Hawaii.

Luckily enough, this is a dream which cannot only be fulfilled by 20-30-year-old super athletes; no - we Masters also have realistic opportunities to make the dream of an Ironman finish to come true for us. The several thousand Masters who take part in currently 20 Ironman events around the world every year are proof of this fact. Many of them meet again in Hawaii at the Kailua-Kona Pier.

Any athlete who admires and envies finishing times of 9 and 10 hours in the Ironman distance, and has problems with his own motivation as a result of this, should take an urgent look at comparable finishing times which I have calculated using age coefficients. I hope that this will help you also to increase your motivation for training. Even if it's only a numerical puzzle, it shows those Master finishing times of over 12, 13 or 14 hours in their true light.

Using the age coefficients according to CEPELKA, Master performances are comparable with those by top-class athletes.

Age	Age Coefficient	8:00h	9:00h	10:00h	11:00h	12:00h
27	1.0000	8:00	9:00	10:00	11:00	12:00
30	0.9927	8:04	8:04	10:05	11:05	12:06
35	0.9690	8:16	9:18	10:20	11:22	12:24
40	0.9411	8:30	9:34	10:37	11:41	12:45
45	0.9132	8:46	9:52	10:57	12:03	13:09
50	0.8854	9:02	10:10	11:17	12:25	13:33
55	0.8575	9:20	10:30	11:40	12:50	14:00
60	0.8252	9:42	10:55	12:07	13:20	14:33
65	0.7817	10:14	10:31	12:47	14:04	15:21
70	0.7253	11:00	12:23	13:45	15:08	16:30

Table: Performances on the Ironman Distance in relation to age

The following comparisons can be deduced from this table.

An athlete who, at the age of 60, is able to complete the Ironman Distance in 13:20h, has achieved a performance comparable to that of a top-class athlete who manages a finishing time of 11:00h. An Ironman finishing time of 11:17h achieved by a 50-year-old, is comparable to a finishing time of 10:00h for a 26-27-year old athlete.

Due to the smaller proportion of muscle, women receive in general a bonus of 10%.

Ironman = Challenge

Coping with a 140-mile triathlon distance is a great challenge for every athlete. This is not only true for one's first competitive performance at this distance, but rather again and again. The competitions that follow have something special about them. So far in my 20 triathlon years, I have finished no less than 30 Long- and Ironman Distances and I know that one cannot consider a competition to be 'completed' or 'out of the way' beforehand. Nobody manages an Ironman 'in passing'. However don't worry, once you're well prepared you will master the Ironman adventure. Athletes who have already completed several Middle distances and perhaps the odd marathon or two, have, with the right attitude, the best chances of reaching their goal.

If you fulfill both the necessary sporting requirements with, at least three years of regular endurance training as well as those performances indicated later, and you have organized all this to fit in with your personal circumstances, you may then set about planning your Ironman. This planning should already occur in the transitional period. On the long autumn and winter evenings one's anticipation of the oncoming great event can start to grow. Anyone with mental adjustment difficulties may be recommended to heed the brief, simple formula below:

Regard the Ironman distance as an enticing three-course meal:
Starter: 2.4 miles swimming
Main Course: 112 miles cycling
Dessert: 26.2 miles running

What you need now is a strong healthy appetite to manage this meal.

The following recommendations, suggestions, tips and advice will make sure that your appetite is immense.

Before my first Ironman, I spent many months asking myself whether I would manage it at all in the first place. As I constantly tackled distances, which were unthinkable for me at that time, I suddenly came up with the idea of the three-course meal. It was a big help to me on the way towards my firm, resolute "Yes, you will, you will manage it!" It was not until I had mentally got to grips with these 140 miles, and I was sure that I was able to win this battle, that I began with the necessary training.

The big dream now becomes a concrete goal.

From the **dream** to the **goal** and on to the **Ironman**, this is the path that leads to an Ironman finish.

We've all dreamt about it for long enough, so now let's set ourselves a realistic goal.

Realistic Goal Planning

The first step in this great challenge is to plan our goals. We have to set our goal by taking our previous competition performances as well as our own individual circumstances into consideration. There are many possibilities here. Our wishes and dreams can spread from merely finishing, to a targeted finishing time, to a qualifying placement for Hawaii, up to winning in one's age category.

We Masters in particular however, should be honest to ourselves and should not build castles in the air. We have to keep our two feet firmly on the ground. The first commandment here is to 'finish'. This is still my main aim today. However even with finishing as the main goal, there are, due to our individual talent, our characteristics and the opportunities available to us, large differences which are particularly noticeable over 140 miles.

In order to deal with the entire performance spectrum for Masters, I would like to indicate the following four areas in the upcoming training recommendations.

a)   14-15 hours
b)   12-13 hours
c)   10-11 hours
d)   Under 10 hours

Many Masters can manage to complete the magical 140 miles in a finishing time of 12-13 hours, sometimes even 11 hours, in their very first competition of this kind. A necessity is systematic endurance training and a suitable all-round situation. In the training plans that follow we can see that one's age is a decisive factor for the amount of time invested. However, I don't mean using any 'off-the-peg plans', but rather those training plans, which have been carried out and their intensity proved. The results of training will be able to be seen.

In order to tackle the 10-hour-mark or even go under it, one generally requires a considerably higher amount of training, good sporting opportunities, an extra portion of stamina, willpower, endurance ability, many years of experience and an all-round positive situation. An example for this is Kalli NOTTRODT. Between 40 and 50 years of age he still managed to achieve finishing times that were well under the 10-hour-mark. More on this later.

Masters who still go out to work every day, have a young family to support and then, as well as this, take part in a triathlon, have to go about planning their training in a completely different way to those who are now retired and whose children are already grown-up, as these have simply much more time to devote to their hobby. For the first group, in which all the younger Masters are bound to be, I have already illustrated how one can minimize the time strain factor through training in Chapter 2 - 'Partner-friendly Training':

The following recommendations apply to a general Ironman competition. It could be a qualifying competition. Planning and suggestions given refer to the last six months before the Ironman. Those who then qualify for Ironman Hawaii are advised to have a three-week regeneration phase with light training only and a similar new build-up for Day X in Hawaii. Due to the extreme weather conditions one can expect to achieve times, which, for Masters, are 30-40 minutes faster than in the qualifying competitions. Lanzarote is an exception here because of its very difficult cycling route.

Training Volume and Requirements for 14-15h and 12-13h

What **requirements** should be **fulfilled**, in order to be able to achieve a target time of 14-15 and 12-13 hours?

Aim	14-15h	12-13h
Swimming 2 000yds	50-55 min	45-48 min
Cycling 56 miles	3:20h/16mph	3:10h/17,5 mph
10km	53-54 min	47 min
Half-distance	2.00h	1.44h
Marathon 13.1 miles		
Marathon 26.2 miles	4.12h	3.40h

Approximate Individual Times Necessary in Competition

Aim	14-15h	12-13h
Swimming	1:50h - 2:00h	1:30h
Cycling	7:30h	6:30h
Running	5:15h	4:30h

Training Volume in the last Six Months before the Ironman

Training volume in the last six months	14-15h	12-13h
Swimming	78,000yds = 3,000yds per week	91,000yds = 3,500yds per week
Cycling	1,900mi = 73mi per week	2,200mi = 85mi per week
Running	625mi = 24mi per week	690mi = 26mi per week
Amount of training required per week (pure training time)	10 hours per week + Stretching exercises	11 hours per week + Stretching exercises

Training In The Transitional Period

October, November, December, January

▲ 2x a week relaxed trot for 1-1:15h each.

▲ 1-2x a week relaxed swimming, perhaps a relaxed cycle.

▲ Analysis of the previous season, planning of new season.

Training In The Preparation Period

February, March, April, May

▲ Basic training; focus on running + swimming, perhaps relaxed cycle.

▲ At the beginning of the first part of the preparation period, training volume increases at low intensity, heart rates 120-130.

▲ Make use of cross-country skiing opportunities to work on arm and trunk muscles.

January:

▲ Running approx. 25-30 miles per week
▲ Steady continuous runs with pulse 120-130
▲ 1x a week, long, calm run of 13-16 miles
▲ Occasional participation in fun runs, 90%
▲ In dry weather 1-1:30h cycling
▲ Swimming 3 000yds per week

February: swimming month

▲ Motto here is to swim as often as possible
▲ E.g. 3x 1 500 - 3 000yds
▲ Where possible with training instructor
▲ 1x a week endurance 2x 1 000yds, see swimming workouts Chapter 6
▲ Running: 1x 8 miles, 1x 12 miles

March: running month

▲ Normal swimming training
▲ Cycling trips at the weekends, 40-45 miles easy pedalling.
▲ 100 rpm, take the bike to work.
▲ Central focus is running training, goal is perhaps a marathon, see running training (37-44 miles), don't neglect stretching exercises!

April: cycling month

▲ Swimming: 3 000-4 000yds per week
▲ Running: 20-25 miles per week
▲ After the marathon only relaxed running allowed for two weeks. Cycling training has priority. At weekends, rounded pedalling with the small chain gear is practiced. Be sure to have 100-110 rpm., e.g Fridays 35 miles, Saturdays 50 miles + 4 miles run, Sundays 62 miles, Wednesdays 30 miles. Athletes with the opportunity to go on a training holiday, should make use of this chance. Volume 600-700 miles in two weeks are a good base. As well as this 2-3x 1h relaxed running

May:

▲ At the weekends practice cycle-run transition, in each case one session relaxed, the other session brisk, e.g. 50 miles cycling + 6 miles running; 35 miles cycling + 13 miles running. 1x per week intervals on the bike, e.g. 3 miles tempo, 3 miles calm, 3 miles tempo...; 2 x 6 miles with 85-90% intensity in each case.

▲ Normal, normal and regenerative training weeks alternately, NNR. Young Masters can also do NNNR. Swimming as in the previous month, intervals, 1x continuous method. Running: 1x a week interval training or FL, e.g. 1 000yds relaxed trot in each case until pulse has reached 110; 2 x 5 000yds 85%, 10 minute break, relaxed trotting. Running volume 25-30 miles, very important is the 16-18 mile long run every two weeks; see Running Training Chapter 4. End of May: short triathlon as test competition

Training in the Competition Period: End of May - October

June, July: see detailed training plans

▲ 14-15h Aim: see training plans
▲ 12-13h Aim: see training plans

At the beginning of June perhaps a middle triathlon to check overall form

With all the physical preparation do not neglect mental training!

July/August: IRONMAN

Congratulations to all finishers! Wasn't it a great experience? Let's go for another one next year!

Every finisher has now earned his regeneration phase. This means a relaxing 3-4 weeks with light training only, despite the even greater motivation now. Time to catch up on all those things that have been neglected in the last while

September: After 2-3 normal training weeks 1-2 Short or Middle triathlon competitions to round off the season

Training Emphasis: Middle Distance Competition

Date: from _____ until _____ week: 1

Day	Weight lbs (a.m.)	S Dist. yds	S Time	C Dist. mi	C Time	R Dist. mi	R Time	Other sporting activity	Comment	Pulse Rest/Strain	Weight (p.m.)
Mon.								Stretching exercises*			
Tues.				50	Calm	5	brisk	*	Combi-training C + R		
Wed.		1,800	Interv.								
Thur.				35	Relaxed	8	Trot	*			
Fri.		1,000	Endur.								
Sat.									Check bike		
Sun.		2,200		56		13		*	Middle Triathlon 6:30h-6:40h		
Total:		5,000		141		26					

Training Emphasis: Regeneration

Date: from _____ until _____ week: 2

Day	Weight lbs (a.m.)	S Dist. yds	Time	C Dist. mi	Time	R Dist. mi	Time	Other sporting activity	Comment	Pulse Rest/ Strain	Weight (p.m.)
Mon.				16	Very calm						
Tues.						6	Calm	*			
Wed.		2,000	Endur.								
Thur.											
Fri.		1,500	Interv.								
Sat.				50	Relaxed						
Sun.						11	Relaxed	*			
Total:		3,500		66		17					

Training Emphasis: Swimming and Cycling

Date: from   **until**   **week: 3**

Day	Weight lbs (a.m.)	S Dist. yds	Time	C Dist. mi	Time	R Dist. mi	Time	Other sporting activity	Comment	Pulse Rest/ Strain	Weight (p.m.)
Mon.											
Tues.				25	Relaxed	9	FL	*	Combi-training C + R		
Wed.		2 000	Interv.								
Thur.				50				*	C: 4x3 miles brisk		
Fri.						15	Calm	*			
Sat.				60	Brisk						
Sun.		3 000	Endur.								
Total:		5 000		135		24					

Training Emphasis: Running and Cycling

Date: from ___ until ___   week: 4

Day	Weight lbs (a.m.)	S Dist. yds	S Time	C Dist. mi	C Time	R Dist. mi	R Time	Other sporting activity	Comment	Pulse Rest/Strain	Weight (p.m.)
Mon.											
Tues.				30	Calm	11	Quick	*	R:5x1,000m TT		
Wed.		2,500	Interv.	37	Brisk						
Thur.						16	Calm	*			
Fri.											
Sat.				80	Calm	6	Relaxed	*	Combi-traininng C + R		
Sun.		2,000	Endur.								
Total:		4,500		147		33					

Training Emphasis: Swimming

Date: from   until

Day	Weight lbs (a.m.)	S Dist. yds	Time	C Dist. mi	Time	R Dist. mi	Time	Other sporting activity	Comment	Pulse Rest/Strain	Weight (p.m.)
Mon.											
Tues.				25	Calm	9	FL	*			
Wed.		2,500	Interv.								
Thur.		3,000	Endur.								
Fri.				37	Brisk sections			*			
Sat.				60	Relaxed						
Sun.		2,000	Interv.			13	Calm	*			
Total:		7,500		122		22					

Training Emphasis: Ironman Distance

Date: from   until   week: 6

Day	Weight lbs (a.m.)	S Dist. yds	Time	C Dist. mi	Time	R Dist. mi	Time	Other sporting activity	Comment	Pulse Rest/Strain	Weight (p.m.)
Mon.											
Tues.				25	Calm	8		*	R: 2mi brisk		
Wed.		1,500	Relaxed								
Thur.				20	Calm			*			
Fri.											
Sat.		3,800		112		26.2			Ironman 14-15h		
Sun.				15	very calm						
Total:		1,500 + 3 800		60 + 112		8 + 26.2		***	Best of luck. You're bound to succeed!		

A word of explanation: While adhering to the training principles already mentioned you must alter these training recommendations to fit in with your own personal circumstances. The recommendations indicated can and should only be a guide.

Training Emphasis: Test Competition, Middle Distance

Date: from _____ until _____ week: 1

Day	Weight lbs (a.m.)	S Dist. yds	S Time	C Dist. mi	C Time	R Dist. mi	R Time	Other sporting activity	Comment	Pulse Rest/Strain	Weight (p.m.)
Mon.		2,500	Interv.					Stretching exercises*			
Tues.				60	Brisk	6	Calm	*			
Wed.				35	Relaxed						
Thur.						8	Relaxed	*			
Fri.		2,000	Endur.								
Sat.											
Sun.		2,200		56		13		*	Middle Distance		
Total:		4,500 + 2,200		95 + 56		14 + 13					

Training Emphasis: Regeneration

Date: from   **until**   **week: 2**

Day	Weight lbs (a.m.)	S Dist. yds	Time	C Dist. mi	Time	R Dist. mi	Time	Other sporting activity	Comment	Pulse Rest/ Strain	Weight (p.m.)
Mon.									*		
Tues.				30	Calm						
Wed.		2,000	Endur.			8	Calm	*			
Thur.											
Fri.						11	Calm	*			
Sat.				.50	Relaxed						
Sun.		1,500	Interv.								
Total:		3,500		80		19					

Training Emphasis: Regeneration/Cycling

Date: from   until   week: 3

Day	Weight lbs (a.m.)	S Dist. yds	S Time	C Dist. mi	C Time	R Dist. mi	R Time	Other sporting activity	Comment	Pulse Rest/ Strain	Weight (p.m.)
Mon.											
Tues.				25	Relaxed	8	FL	*	Combin. Training C + R		
Wed.		2,000	Interv.								
Thur.				40	FL						
Fri.						16	Calm	*			
Sat.				60	Brisk						
Sun.		2,500	Endur.			6	Relaxed	*			
Total:		4,500		125		30					

Training Emphasis: Cycling and Running

week: 4

Date: from ___ until ___

Day	Weight lbs (a.m.)	S Dist. yds	S Time	C Dist. mi	C Time	R Dist. mi	R Time	Other sporting activity	Comment	Pulse Rest/Strain	Weight (p.m.)
Mon.											
Tues.				30	Relaxed	11	Quick	*	R: 5x1,000m TT		
Wed.		2,500	Interv.	25	FL						
Thur.						16	Calm	*			
Fri.				37	Calm						
Sat.				80	Relaxed	6	FL	*	Combi-training C+R		
Sun.		2,500	Endur.								
Total:		5,000		172		33					

Training Emphasis: Swimming

Date: from   until   week: 5

Day	Weight lbs (a.m.)	S		C		R		Other sporting activity	Comment	Pulse Rest/ Strain	Weight (p.m.)
		Dist. yds	Time	Dist. mi	Time	Dist. mi	Time				
Mon.		2,000	Interv.								
Tues.				35	Relaxed	8	Brisk	*			
Wed.		2,400	Interv.								
Thur.						11	Calm	*			
Fri.				45	Brisk						
Sat.		3,000	Endur.								
Sun.						13	Very calm	*			
Total:		7,400		80		32					

Training Emphasis: Ironman Distance/Competition

Date: from   until   week: 6

Day	Weight lbs (a.m.)	S Dist. yds	S Time	C Dist. mi	C Time	R Dist. mi	R Time	Other sporting activity	Comment	Pulse Rest/ Strain	Weight (p.m.)
Mon.											
Tues.				25	Relaxed						
Wed.		1,500	Relaxed			9		*	R: 3 000m very brisk		
Thur.				20	Calm						
Fri.											
Sat.											
Sun.		3,800		112		26.2		***	Ironman 12-13h		
Total:		1,500 + 3 800		45 + 112		9 + 26.2			Have fun, finisher! Well done!		

A word of explanation: While adhering to the training principles already mentioned you must alter these training recommendations to fit in with your own personal circumstances. The recommendations indicated can and should only be a guide.

What requirements should be fulfilled, in order to be able to achieve a target time of 10-11h and under 10 hours?

Aim	10-11h	< 10h
Swimming 2,000yds	38-40 min	< 35 min
Cycling 56 miles	2:30h/22mph	2:22h/24 mph
6 miles	38 min	34-35 min
Half-distance		
Marathon 13.1 miles	1:27h	1:18h
Marathon 26.2 miles	3:00-3:10h	2:45-2:50h

Approximate Individual Times necessary in Competition

Aim	10-11h	< 10h
Swimming	1:10-1:15h	1:00h
Cycling	5:30h	5:10h
Running	3:50-4:00h	3:20h

Training Volume in the Last Six Months before Ironman

Training volume in the last six months	10-11h	< 10h
Swimming	88mi = 3-4mi per week	125-250mi = 5-10mi per week
Cycling	3-4,000mi = 130mi per week	3,700 - 5,000mi = 170mi per week
Running	815mi = 31mi	1 000mi = 38-40mi
Amount of training required per week (pure training time)	12-14h per week + stretching exercises	15-20h per week + stretching exercises

The Annual Schedule

Transitional Period: November, December, perhaps January

▲ Recovery, mental and physical.

▲ 2-3x a week relaxed running 8-9 miles, relaxed swimming without the stopwatch. Analysis of the previous season, suggestions for improvement and planning of the upcoming competition period.

Preparation Period: January - mid May

▲ **Basic endurance training.**

At the beginning of the first half of the preparation period, training volume increases at low intensity. Heart rates 130. In order to work on arm and trunk muscles, one should make use of any cross-country skiing opportunities. Stretching exercises and strength training support the overall blood circulation in the body.

▲ **Running:** 3-4x a week; 30-40 miles, or 45-50 miles.

Steady continuous runs. A long, calm run per week of 16-19 miles with pulse 130.

▲ **Cycling Training:** In dry weather 1-1:30h, perhaps the roller 2x 45 min.

▲ **Stretching:** 3x 20 min

▲ **Swimming:** 3-4x technique + intervals + continuous swimming

See swimming workouts Chapter 6.

February: perhaps swimming month.

As well as normal training, one goes swimming as often as possible. Volume: considerably higher than the rest of the other parts of the season.

Important!: Every third week should be for regeneration with low intensity and volume.

Cycling trips in dry weather.

March: perhaps running month.

▲ **Normal swimming training:** 3-4 miles per week, or 5-10 miles per week for those aiming for < 10 hours. Stretching exercises, keep up strength training.

▲ **Cycling training:** Easy pedalling in cycling sessions with 110 rpm and small chain gear.

Prepare for April, the cycling month. Include cycling training in marathon preparation.

Emphasis: Running with the aim of a marathon run in 3:00h or 3:10h at the end of March/ beginning of April.

Training instructions in Chapter 4 - Running Training.

April: perhaps cycling month.

Alternative: March-cycling month/February running month/ January-swimming month. Perhaps cut down swimming 2-3 miles, or 4-6 miles for Ironman < 10h.

▲ **Running:** After a successful marathon two weeks of relaxed training 2 x 9 miles, then normal training again.

▲ **Cycling:** Emphasis at wekends and on holidays. If possible a two-week training block in warmer regions with 800 miles cycling and 50 miles running in two weeks.

Work on rounded pedalling and basic endurance. During this time relaxed swimming and running only. See training tips in Chapter 5.

May:

At the weekends combination training.

Brisk cycling session (50-60 miles) + calm 8-12 mile run. Calm cycling training (75-95 miles) + brisk 5-mile run.

▲ **Swimming:** As well as interval training, head for open waters for contnuous training.

▲ **Running:** 45-50 miles 1x a week interval training, e.g. 2-3 x 3 miles, 6 x 500yds, using 500/1,000/2,000/1,000/500yard speed intervals with 500yds relaxed trot in between.

Competition Period: Mid-May – Mid-October

▲ Stabilisation of best form.

▲ Specific competition training.

▲ Cut down loads in the last 10-12 days before the competition. Take part in 1-2 short/middle triathlons in the run-up to the Ironman (see training plans).

▲ Do not underestimate mental training as regards the seasonal highlight.

▲ After competition, be sure to do regeneration for long enough.

▲ Very low loads, days of rest, relaxed training 1x a day only, sauna, massage, enough fluid, minerals, vitamins.

▲ Avoid overtraining caused by too many triathlons.

▲ After an Ironman, three weeks of regeneration, up to 50% training volume with hardly any intensity.

Training Plans for an Ironman in 10-11h

The concrete training plans below stem from practical experience. Henry, 53 years of age, 18th triathlon season. March: 2-week cycling block training. The last three-and-a-half weeks before competition served as a swimming block, as in the six months beforehand a total of only 30 swimming miles had been completed.

The Last Six Weeks before the Ironman

Emphasis: Swimming and Short Triathlon as Test Competition

Date: from 12.6   until 18.6   week: 1 Ironman Training

Day	Weight lbs (a.m.)	S Dist. yds	S Time	C Dist. mi	C Time	R Dist. mi	R Time	Other sporting activity	Comment	Pulse Rest/Strain	Weight (p.m.)
Mon.		2,500 2,500	Lake neopr.			10	Pulse 122				
Tues.				8 + 35							
Wed.				8 + 8		8					
Thur.		1 500				7	Calm		S: no effort		
Fri.						6	Relaxed				
Sat.				25							
Sun.		1,000	0:21	25		6	0:35	2:04h	Short Triathlon, C + R strong		
Total:		7,500		109		37					

Emphasis: Regeneration and long cycles

Date: from 19.6   until 25.6   week: 2 Ironman Training

Day	Weight lbs (a.m.)	S Dist. yds	S Time	C Dist. mi	C Time	R Dist. mi	R Time	Other sporting activity	Comment	Pulse Rest/ Strain	Weight (p.m.)
Mon.											
Tues.											
Wed.				8 + 8		9	1:14			47	
Thur.		2,500	Lake			16	2:05				
Fri.	174.5	2,500	Lake								177.5
Sat.				65	Hilly						
Sun.				55		6	0:41				
Total:		5,000		136		31					

Emphasis: Holiday preparation, long running and cycling sessions at weekend

Date: from 26.6   until 2.7   week: 3 Ironman Training

Day	Weight lbs (a.m.)	S Dist. yds	S Time	C Dist. mi	C Time	R Dist. mi	R Time	Other sporting activity	Comment	Pulse Rest/Strain	Weight (p.m.)
Mon.									No time		
Tues.									No time		
Wed.									No time		
Thur.		2,000	Lake			6	0:52		Holiday at lake		
Fri.		2,000	with necpr.	30		16	2:07		S continuous swims		
Sat.		2,000		65		6	0:54		S with neoprene		
Sun		2,000		90							
Total:		8,000		185		28					

Emphasis: Swimming, running and cycling sessions (Holiday at Lake)

Date: from 26.6   until 2.7   week: 4 Ironman Training

Day	Weight lbs (a.m.)	S Dist. yds	S Time	C Dist. mi	C Time	R Dist. mi	R Time	Other sporting activity	Comment	Pulse Rest/Strain	Weight (p.m.)
Mon.		2,900	Lake						Holiday		
Tues.		2,900	Continuous			17	2:16				
Wed.		1,500				16	2:10				
Thur.		2,900 1 000		50	17.6mph				S always with neopr		
Fri.		2,500	Interv.								
Sat.						22	3.05		R: super/ very relaxed		
Sun.		2,000		70	17mph						
Total:		15,700		120		55					

Emphasis: Long swimming and running sessions, Holiday

Date: from 10.7 **until 16.7** **week: 5 Ironman Training**

Day	Weight lbs (a.m.)	S Dist. yds	S Time	C Dist. mi	C Time	R Dist. mi	R Time	Other sporting activity	Comment	Pulse Rest/Strain	Weight (p.m.)
Mon.		2,000	Lake 0.39	37	20.6				C: tempo		
Tues.											
Wed.		2,900	0:56			19	2:30		S + R really good		
Thur.		2,900	Neopr.								
Fri.		2,900	0:57	53	17mph						
Sat.						16	1:59				176
Sun.	174					6	0:55				
Total:		10,700		90		41					

Emphasis: Ironman, Holiday

Date: from 17.7   **until 23.7**   **week: 6 Ironman Training**

Day	Weight lbs (a.m.)	S Dist. yds	S Time	C Dist. mi	C Time	R Dist. mi	R Time	Other sporting activity	Comment	Pulse Rest/ Strain	Weight (p.m.)
Mon.		2,000		25	Relaxed						
Tues.		2,900	0:54			8	1:13				
Wed.		2,900	0:53	30	17.5mph						
Thur.		2,000	0:39			6	0:53				
Fri.	174										
Sat.		1,500									
Sun.		3,800	1:09	112	5:29	26.2	3:52	10:39:12	Ironman		
Total:		11,300 + 3,800		55 + 112		14 + 26					

In order for you to be able to have a better overall view of the plans, here is some information on my personal circumstances.

Cycling only from the end of February until the end of September. From March onwards, 8 miles daily to work and back on the bike. April: Two weeks training camp with approx. 680 miles cycling and 45 miles running.

Personal shortcomings/ inadequacies:

Spontaneous strength training and stretching exercises only. No cycling from October to February, not even on the roller. All in all not enough swimming training. Not much interval training on the bike or while running.

Personal strengths:

Continuous training, mental strength, very contented feeling as regards competition distribution.

While paying attention to the training principles already mentioned, alter these training recommendations to fit in with your own personal circumstances. The recommendations given can and should only be a guide.

Training Plans for the Hawaii Ironman in 9:48h

Here are some concrete training examples for a finishing time of around nine hours, (9.48 in this case) in the Ironman in Hawaii.

Any Master aiming to finish an Ironman in 9-10 hours must - provided he's not a real professional - be able to combine all his positive influences. Included here are: talent, ability to accomplish what he sets out to do, willpower, good training opportunities, time, ambition, diligence in training, physical and mental strength, motivation. Accordingly he shows himself to have a general performance-enhancing set of personal circumstances. Kalli NOTTRODT is such a person. He is one of the few athletes around the world who, at almost 50, can still manage to finish the Ironman (140 miles) under the 10-hour mark, even in Hawaii. With his performance capabilities he still finishes other Ironman events in 9-9:15 hours.

Some basic information about his training:

Regeneration months: November and December. During winter strength training 2x a week and aerobics/gymnastics 2-3x a week.

His spring training:

From January: emphasis on running (50-60 miles a week) + swimming (9-12 miles a week), cycling only in good weather and at temperatures over +5°. March: 2-week cycling block in sunny regions. In May another ten days cycling block. Average training duration: Nearly 20 hours a week.

Training volume in this season: Swimming: 430 miles

Cycling: 7 200 miles

Running: 1 750 miles

So as to be able to understand Kalli NOTTRODT's training notes, below are some relevant details.

Born in 1952, triathlete since 1984, before that a competitive swimmer with personal best times of 1:09 min for 100m breaststroke and 2:31 min for 200m breaststroke.

1,000m Best Swimming Time: 13:00 min without neoprene
1,500m: 19:30 without neoprene
10,000m Best Running Time: 33:50 min
25 miles Cycling Best Time: 60 min
112 miles cycling: 4:48h
Completed Ironman several times in under nine hours.

Kalli's (48 years old) specific training as preparation for the Hawaii Ironman is as follows:

The Last Six Weeks before Hawaii

Kalli

Date: from 4.9   until 10.9   **week: 1 Ironman Hawaii**

Day	Weight lbs (a.m.)	S Dist. yds	S Time	C Dist. mi	C Time	R Dist. mi	R Time	Other sporting activity	Comment	Pulse Rest/Strain	Weight (p.m.)
Mon.		4,000	1:20	44	2:20	6	0:44				
Tues.		3,100	1:00	35	2:10						
Wed.	159					8	1:00				
Thur.		3,600	1:10	44	2:20	10	1:10				
Fri.				74	4:00	9	1:10		C/R Combin.		
Sat.	161										
Sun.		3,300	1:00	44		8	1.00		C/R Combin.		
Total:		14,000		241		41					

Kalli

Date: from 11.9   until 17.9   week: 2 Ironman Hawaii

Day	Weight lbs (a.m.)	S Dist. yds	Time	C Dist. mi	Time	R Dist. mi	Time	Other sporting activity	Comment	Pulse Rest/Strain	Weight (p.m.)
Mon.		3,800	1:10	58	3.00				C: Intervals 10 x 2 min		
Tues.		3,200	1:00	110	6:00	13	1:30		Hard training, C/R		
Wed.	159	3,200	1:00								
Thur.	161	2,600	0:50	20	1:00	9	1:00				
Fri.	159										
Sat.						10	1:20		Rainy weather		
Sun.				63	4:00	9	1:00		Combin., R quick		
Total:		12,800		251		41					

Kalli

Date: from 18.9   until 24.9   week: 3 Ironman Hawaii

Day	Weight lbs (a.m.)	S		C		R		Other sporting activity	Comment	Pulse Rest/ Strain	Weight (p.m.)
		Dist. yds	Time	Dist. mi	Time	Dist. mi	Time				
Mon.		3,000	1:00								
Tues.	159	1,500	0:30	58	3:00	9	1:00		C: Intervals 12x 2 min		
Wed.		4,000	1:20	56	3:00	9	1:00				
Thur.		4,400	1:30						S: 20 x 100yds		
Fri.	161	2,800	0:50	35	2:00	8	1:00				
Sat.		3,500	1:10	58	3:00	11	1:15				
Sun.	159	2,800	0:50						S: Only relaxed		
Total:		22,000		207		37					

Kalli

Date: from 18.9   until 24.9   week: 4 Ironman Hawaii

Day	Weight lbs (a.m.)	S Dist. yds	S Time	C Dist. mi	C Time	R Dist. mi	R Time	Other sporting activity	Comment	Pulse Rest/ Strain	Weight (p.m.)
Mon.				45	2:30	17	2:10				
Tues.		3,000	1:00	63	3:10	9	1:00		C: 6x12 min tempo		
Wed.	160	4 000	1:30			11	1:15				
Thur.		4,300		44	2:20	4	0:30		C/R Combin., R tempo		
Fri.		3,200	1:00			11	1:15				
Sat.	161								Departure Hawaii		
Sun.		2,000	0:40						Arrival Hawaii		
Total:		16,500		152		52					

Kalli

Date: from 02.10   until 08.10   week: 5 Ironman Hawaii

Day	Weight lbs (a.m.)	S Dist. yds	S Time	C Dist. mi	C Time	R Dist. mi	R Time	Other sporting activity	Comment	Pulse Rest/ Strain	Weight (p.m.)
Mon.		2,500	0:50	44	2:20	6	50		Training in		
Tues.		3,000	0:50	32	2:00	8	60		Hawaii		
Wed.		2,200	0:40								
Thur.		3,200	1:00	69	3:40	7	50				
Fri.		2,200	0:40	39	2:00	8	60				
Sat.		1,800	0:30	73	3:40	6	50				
Sun.		2,000	0:40								
Total:		16,900		257		35					

Kalli

Date: from 09.10   until 15.10   week: 6 Ironman Hawaii

Day	Weight lbs (a.m.)	S Dist. yds	S Time	C Dist. mi	C Time	R Dist. mi	R Time	Other sporting activity	Comment	Pulse Rest/Strain	Weight (p.m.)
Mon.		2,000	0:40								
Tues.		2,000	0:40	27	1:30	4	0:30		C: 6x2min, lactate margin		
Wed.		1,500	0:30	32	2:00	4	0:30		C + R relaxed		
Thur.		500	0:10						S: 20x100		
Fri.				20							
Sat.		**3,800**	**57.12**	**112**	**5:30**	**26.2**	**3:15**		**Ironman Hawaii 9:48h**		
Sun.											
Total:		6,000 + 3,800		79 + 112		8 + 26.2					

A typical week of regeneration in the **winter** looks like this for Kalli:

Kalli – a typical Regeneration Week in Winter

Date: from   until   week:

Day	Weight lbs (a.m.)	S		C		R		Other sporting activity	Comment	Pulse Rest/ Strain	Weight (p.m.)
		Dist. yds	Time	Dist. mi	Time	Dist. mi	Time				
Mon.		2,000	0:40					Tai-Boo			
Tues.		3,000	0:60			6	0:50				
Wed.		2,000	0:40					Spinning			
Thur.											
Fri.		2,000	0:40								
Sat.				37							
Sun.						6	0:50				
Total:		9,000		37		12					

The following shows a typical week of regeneration for Kalli in the **summer**.

Kalli – a typical Regeneration Week in summer

Date: from   until   week:

Day	Weight lbs (a.m.)	S Dist. yds	Time	C Dist. mi	Time	R Dist. mi	Time	Other sporting activity	Comment	Pulse Rest/Strain	Weight (p.m.)
Mon.		2,000	0:40	37	2:00	6	0:50				
Tues.		2,000	0:40								
Wed.		3,000	1:00								
Thur.				37	2:00	6	0:50				
Fri.		2,000	0:40	44	2:30						
Sat.		3,000	1:00	37	2:00	4	0:30				
Sun.											
Total:		12,000		155		16					

I would now like to show you my training for a finishing time of 9:55h as a comparison.

I achieved this at the Ironman Europe at the age of 46.

Training Plans for the Ironman Europe in 9:55h

The last five weeks before the Ironman Europe.

▲ Henry, 46 years old, 11th triathlon season.

▲ From March 11 miles cycling daily to work.

▲ In March a two-week cycling block

▲ Weekly amount of training in mid-year: 13.8 hours.

Emphasis: Triathlon Middle Distance

Date: from 7.6   until 13.6   week: 1

Day	Weight lbs (a.m.)	S Dist. yds	S Time	C Dist. mi	C Time	R Dist. mi	R Time	Other sporting activity	Comment	Pulse Rest/Strain	Weight (p.m.)
Mon		2,000	Lake, neopr.	11 27		11	1:16		Hot, complete apathy		
Tues									Apathy	52	
Wed		2,000		11 27		11	1:30		Apathy		
Thurs				46	17mph				Apathy		
Fri				11 11					Apathy	46	
Sat		2,000	0:37 neop.	50	2:20h 21.4 mph	12.5	1:20	Was good fun	Middle Distance 4:22h		
Sun											
Total:		6,000		194		34.5					

Emphasis: Regeneration and Long Cycles

Date: from 14.06   until 20.06   week: 2

Day	Weight lbs (a.m.)	S Dist. yds	S Time	C Dist. mi	C Time	R Dist. mi	R Time	Other sporting activity	Comment	Pulse Rest/Strain	Weight (p.m.)
Mon											
Tues				16 20		8					
Wed				11 11		8					
Thurs				11 11							
Fri	173	2,000	Lake			16	2:00				177.5
Sat				97	5:10						
Sun		1,500	0:40	25		6	0:50		Short Triathlon 90%		
Total:		3,500		202		38					

Emphasis: Swimming and Cycling

Date: from 21.06   until 27.06   week: 3

Day	Weight lbs (a.m.)	S Dist. yds	S Time	C Dist. mi	C Time	R Dist. mi	R Time	Other sporting activity	Comment	Pulse Rest/ Strain	Weight (p.m.)
Mon.				11							
Tues.		2,000	10x 200	37 / 11 / 11		8			R: hard		
Wed.				11 / 11		8					
Thur.		3,800	1:14	11 / 11					S: test with neoprene	47	
Fri.		3,800	1:12	11 / 11		9	1:12		S: test with neoprene		
Sat.				77	18.2mph						
Sun.						19	2:14			133	
Total:		9,600		213		44			Hard training week		

Emphasis: Swimming, Running and Cycling, Holiday

Date: from 28.06 until 04.07 **week: 4**

Day	Weight lbs (a.m.)	S Dist. yds	S Time	C Dist. mi	C Time	R Dist. mi	R Time	Other sporting activity	Comment	Pulse Rest/Strain	Weight (p.m.)
Mon.		3,000	Lake, neopr.	37 / 44							
Tues.				11 / 25		8					
Wed.		2,000	Lake			8					
Thur.						8					
Fri.		3,000	Lake	11 / 25							
Sat.						16	2:00				
Sun.				75	3:52						
Total:		8,000		228		40					

Emphasis: Ironman Europe

Date: from 05.07   **until** 11.07   **week: 5**

Day	Weight lbs (a.m.)	S Dist. yds	S Time	C Dist. mi	C Time	R Dist. mi	R Time	Other sporting activity	Comment	Pulse Rest/ Strain	Weight (p.m.)
Mon.				16							
				11							
Tues.				11		4					
Wed.		3,000	Lake, neopr.	28		8					
Thur.											
Fri.											
Sat.		3,800	1:07 +5	112	5:13 +2	26.2	3:28		Rain, cold	Ironman 9:55:01h	
Sun.	78.8								Terrific!		
Total:		3,000 + 3,800		66 + 112		12 + 26.2					

With a similar amount of training I finished the Ironman in Hawaii in 10:44h.

CHAPTER 10

It's not Going to Work without Training Principles

With all the detailed training planning and organization, it's important not to lose one's overall perspective. The most important training principles may be helpful here and these are summarized below. The most common training errors should be totally avoided: too much, too often, too fast, not critical enough as regards our own body and our own individual circumstances.

Training is taboo when one has a high temperature or pains in the chest. When taking private and working stress into consideration as well as any strain on the family, it is important to heed the following:

▲ Triathlon competitions imply working with each other and not against each other or a fight.
▲ Never train for all you're worth, it should always be fun.
▲ Always have the right dosage of training.
▲ Wear the correct running shoes.
▲ React in time to any signals your body gives you.
▲ Do not overtax cooled-down muscles.
▲ Carry out stretching exercises regularly.
▲ Select the correct frame height for your bike.
▲ Allow your body the rest breaks it needs.
▲ Train regularly.
▲ Devote more time in training to your weakest discipline, preferably in a group.
▲ Increase training slowly.
▲ Raise training volume first and then intensity.
▲ Don't just include regenerative measures into training plans but also carry them out as well.
▲ Be well-prepared for training blocks.
▲ Have a balanced diet - as much protein as possible and little fat.
▲ Always listen to your body signals. In this way you develop a good feeling for the right amount of exertion in training and in competition.

- ▲ Take smaller injuries seriously.
- ▲ Always have variety in your training programs.
- ▲ Plan in enough days of rest.
- ▲ Never see training plans as a dogma. Always take account of your strain as a whole, i.e. career, family and sport.
- ▲ The longer the training unit, the less intensive the training must be.
- ▲ An intensive running session should be followed by a relaxed cycling or swimming session, as both involve less strain on our locomotor system.
- ▲ For the Middle and Ironman distances, emphasis training is in the fourth to the second week before the competition.
- ▲ In the last week before the triathlon competition, training should only be relaxed, easy-going, regenerative and low in volume.
- ▲ Begin with food and drink intake early enough in training and competition.
- ▲ Drink plenty on the last day before a competition, eat in moderate amounts.
- ▲ On the morning of the Race Day rub in waterproof suncream, protection factor 30. However be sure to leave out the forehead when doing this.
- ▲ Only use tested materials in competition. This holds for food, drinks and equipment.
- ▲ Triathlon competitions are often decided in one's head, therefore show off your mental strength.
- ▲ When changing location you should devote the third day to active rest.
- ▲ Do not become a swim-cycle-runner who only has sport, sport, sport in his head.
- ▲ Do not become a training champion with only hard training on the agenda with little regeneration and high training volumes. An athlete who checks every heart rate, subjects himself to enormous pressure, carries out his training with toughness and grim determination ruins his private and working life.

▲ Athletes have three lives: a family life, a working life and a sporting life.

▲ As already explained earlier, Masters who have already turned 60 should avoid exertion of over 85% of their maximum pulse.

CHAPTER 11

The Day Has finally Come!

The Last Two Days before the Ironman

One should arrive at the venue **two days** before the Ironman at the latest to be able to calmly carry out the extensive preparations. Anyone who thinks that he will be able to sort everything out on the day before the competition is very much mistaken. The stress and hectic pace rob him of all the energy he has built up, thus reducing his chances of success. Athletes who need to do a relaxing run over 3 miles in his competition socks and shoes or go on a 16 miles relaxing cycle to calm themselves them down should do so. However I would like to warn against having a quick try-out of the cycling distance within a group. This often turns into a mad rush as you want to, or feel you have to, show the other competitors what you're made of. A relaxing cycling trip for young high-performance athletes can be a bolting speed race for a Master.

The obligatory pasta party in the evening gives you the opportunity to meet friends and prepare for the upcoming big day at a calm, easy-going pace. One should not forget to keep drinking the whole day.

The last day before the Ironman is completely booked out with organizational and checking tasks as well as the laying out of competition clothing and equipment. Starting off with the swimming gear, and then the extensive cycling equipment on to the running gear and running shoes, one must test the functional abilities of all the various pieces of equipment. You should take a good two hours for the bike check-in. At the same time you have the chance to get familiar with the transition zone. Many triathletes have wandered around aimlessly in the transition zone because they hadn't thought about this concrete situation intensively enough beforehand. With more than 1,000 competitors, the transition zone is bound to be somewhat confusing. Because the foreseeable weather conditions one can adjust time schedules and in the case of colder weather, have warmer sports clothing ready if necessary.

Only light foods are eaten and we adhere to our normal drinking habits. No alcohol, coffee or tea. Go to bed early enough as the alarm-clock will be waking you at 4 o'clock in the morning. Sex is not 'damaging' here; it is more likely to calm you down.

The Magical Day - The Race Day

At last the day has come. The big day. The day we have long been waiting for. The day which we have planned, trained for and prepared for as best as possible for so long. It will be a strange day for all athletes. A day which one doesn't experience many hundreds of times, but only once, twice or three times in a sporting year.

My own personal perception and experience may be of interest and assistance here in order to give, not only the reader, but also the potential Ironman an impression of the extreme conditions in Hawaii. For this reason I describe my individual problems and difficulties as well as my thoughts and feelings throughout the 140-mile adventure. These enable you to get a detailed view of the overall competition and of an Ironman's feelings and mental state.

The magical day, this long awaited day, the Race day, my unforgettable adventure starts off at four o'clock in the morning. Three hours before the start at Kailua-Kona, I begin the day with a few gymnastic exercises and the usual pre-competition breakfast: muesli, bread with honey, bread with sugar-beet syrup. It has to be rich in carbohydrate and not too hard on the stomach. Along with this my power- drink, made up of Brottrunk, apple juice and water.

The sea is nice and calm at this hour. Swimming is actually the discipline that I dislike. This is completely different in Hawaii though. My beloved marathon run suddenly turns into a discipline to be hated, the otherwise dreaded swimming distance is my favorite discipline all of a sudden.

I felt very comfortable in the 80° F warm waters of the Pacific in the last few days, although I found the swimming training in the weeks at home up to this to be extremely difficult. I definitely have the deserved respect for the 26.2 mile marathon. This is because of the extreme heat, the high humidity levels, and the damned monotony of the lava desert. There are absolutely no thoughts of giving up in these early hours or are they just consciously being banished? I want to finish, i.e. manage to get through it all, this is my commanding order. All in all, I hope for a good finishing time in this my second Ironman, provided everything runs as normal.

But what is normal here in Big Island? I've been here for a week now and have not been able to get an hour of deep sleep. "Hopefully I don't get tired after a few hours," I remark to my wife with a feeling of uncertainty. "There's no point worrying about that now Henry, this is how you wanted it to be."

"I know, this is exactly what I wanted. If only I didn't have to get up so damned early in the morning though," I add feebly. I'm here and I'm going to do my best today, and that's the end of it. So there! The main thing is to finish. The most important thing is to finish; I hope the bike will hold out, the kicking around in the water won't be too extreme, the weather won't be too hot, the Mumuku wind behaves itself. A thousand thoughts fly through my head on this morning. To finish, this is what we all wish each other. Seldom in my life have I heard wishes that were so genuine.

I am fully convinced that these words of greeting are honestly meant. Every competitor knows too well how much training is required in order to be able to tackle the Ironman here.

At 5:30 am we go to the 'Start Check-In'.

The tension is indescribable.

It is still dark. Swarms of athletes and assistants head towards Kailua-Kona pier. Thousands of spectators come together here. I get into conversation with several athletes, we all end up saying

'Good luck! Best of luck!'. The seats on the stand are occupied from early on. The spectators are standing and sitting on the quay walls and waiting patiently. We athletes get our starting numbers written on both of our upper ams and both thighs. The bicycle tires are pumped up to 9 bar/130.5 lbs/sq.in. Full drinking bottles are mounted onto the bike. I tape four energy bars onto my bicycle frame.

The entire start and finishing area is lit up. TV companies are broadcasting this sensation. The many provisional toilet facilities are in frequent use. There is a hustle and bustle here on the pier - still in darkness. The high waves hit against the quay wall, spraying on-lookers, assistants and athletes. If only I was already back here again - ah no, I want to experience a good bit first. A good bit indeed - these are spontaneous thoughts that I have. I have the mythical Ironman 'bull' before my eyes, he has to be tamed today.

More and more athletes, about 80% men and 20% women gather at the Kailua-Kona pier, in total 1 400 athletes in good training form. A huge amount of people. A look at the clock tells me that it's 6:50 am. Ten minutes to go. I put my T-shirt and shoes into a plastic bag with my starting number on it. I quickly rub oil one more time into any chafing spots of the body, give my patient wife one last kiss, and then head off towards the water. At the same time I can enjoy the first rays of sunlight which appear over the surrounding volcanoes and I enter the warm water with a happy feeling of anticipation.

All these hundreds of triathletes, this is what it must be like in an ant hill. Five minutes before the start all suddenly goes quiet among the athletes and spectators. The obligatory prayer before the start - a stirring moment. I sense my inner gratitude, to be al-lowed to experience this here today, at the same time I hope for strength, endurance, mental and physical energy to be able to survive this upcoming adventure.

In the meantime the American national anthem can be heard from all the speakers, I get goose pimples from this. The motto now is 'only' to put into practice all what I have practiced over many months, in countless hours of training in water, on the bike and on foot, and cover these 140 miles swimming, cycling and running. Not child's play by any means, but with some luck, definitely manageable.

My personal three-course-triathlon meal today is as following:

▲ 2.4 miles of swimming in the Pacific Ocean
▲ 112 miles of cycling in Big Island's desert of lava
▲ a 26.2 mile marathon

It will be 'served' to me in a couple of minutes.

All triathletes set their stopwatches to zero and, within the jostling, look for the most favorable starting position possible. We shake each other's hands one more time and wish each other 'a finish' from the bottom of our hearts. Another moving moment. The helicopters with the TV cameras inside soar above the crowd. The countdown begins, many athletes wave and cheer, count along as well. Then one more minute, another 30 seconds, 20, 10, a rumbling of guns, OFF WE GO.

Yellow and red swimming caps tear off like a crowd of hungry wolves. As if they wanted to plough their way through the Pacific Ocean. The sea is bubbling over, the most turbulent swimming miles lie ahead of us. 2 800 arms and 2 800 legs are all in simultaneous movement. Churning water surrounds me, frothy and filled with bubbles. Me, Henry, a moderate swimmer in amongst 1,400 muscle-men.

In between the many arms and legs and at a depth of only a few yards we have entire shoals of fish accompanying us on our way. They probably pity us for our impetuous swimming style, I suddenly think. The uneven, blackish-greenish sea bed - for me personally not particularly appealing - can be seen so clearly from a depth of a few yards and this distracts somewhat from the endless arm and leg movements.

It is practically impossible to swim normally for the first 1,000yds. After that though, I try as much as possible to swim at my speed in these pleasantly warm waters of the Pacific. Calm, even swimming is the motto here, just don't give too much too soon. A long, long day is still ahead of us. I swim past the two Polynesian boats, which are about 1.2 miles from the pier, still within a crowd but without any difficulties. On the way back I am hardly able to make out where the finish is, so I try to get in line and swim in the middle of a wide band of swimmers. Hopefully I can correct my direction here. Who is taking the ideal route here? Probably only those professional swimmers up at the front, I comfort myself. So, I'll just keep on swimming calmly and without too much of a hectic pace. I'm not going to waste all my energy here in the Pacific.

I deliberately take the Triathlon Breakfast of 2.4 swimming miles calmly, without any problems. After a good deal of confusion I can suddenly recognize the finish in the distance. My thoughts are already on the 112 mile cycling route.

I swim on calmly and evenly and reach today's first finish. I'm not satisfied with my time of 1:24h. I had secretly expected it be about 1:20h. Just stay calm, the day is going to be very, very long. I walk, slightly wobbly, through timekeeping up to the transition zone. I shower off the saltwater. Assistants give me my bag of clothes, I dry off, change my clothes, and put on my cycling jersey, cycling shorts, socks, cycling shoes, gloves and helmet. Everything's running like clockwork so far. Keen and avid assistants rub in cream to protect me from the intensive sunlight to be expected. I run to my bike, other assistants pass it to me, Yep, it's the right one. At the marked position I hop up onto my bike and cycle through thousands of spectators with a high rpm and briefly recognize my wife who is kindly calling out to me: "Good going Henry!" And yet again I have needed nearly five minutes for this transition, oh well!

I feel top fit, I'm ready for the desert and the next 112 miles. During the first few miles I immediately overtake a number of athletes. My growing euphoria is strengthened even more by this. Now comes the main course of my three-course triathlon meal, the 112 mile cycling stretch. Slipstream cycling, which is normal for cycling races, is generally forbidden in triathlon and any athlete who doesn't heed this regulation will be disqualified. Crowds of frenzied spectators cheer us up the first hills. Then it's out into the shadeless lava desert. The turning point is 56 miles out of Kona as far as Hawi. I am familiar with the first 30 miles from the many training sessions as well as from my last start. After that come steep uphill sections and the almost constant Mumuku wind, which is up there on the northern part of the island. This Mumuku wind is your worst enemy on the cycling route, as it's very unpredictable and is always particularly strong at that moment when you could really do without it. Big Island, in general, has a lot of wind on offer. In the mornings there are mostly down-draught winds which sweep down from the tops of the volcanoes along the open Highway 19. Just the very spot where we triathletes are at this instant. In between, you have strong sideward breezes coming from some valleys in the distance, and later on the Mumuku is lurking for those athletes who are a good bit further back.

I'm cycling at a good speed, along the west coast of Hawaii under the over 4,000m-high plus Mauna Kea volcano. I have already emptied both of my drinks on the first three miles and take a first bite from my energy bar. My slogan here when cycling is drink, drink and drink again. I have planned to take a new drinks bottle, 0.5l in volume, at every drinks stand, finish this over the 5 miles that follow and exchange it again for a full one. This means taking on 500ml fluid every 15 minutes.With a few exceptions I have managed to keep this up and thus I drink 2 liters of fluid per hour: water and an electrolyte drink alternately.

I have a light headwind on the first 12-18 miles. The hills on these well-built roads, which are practically free of traffic today, are long, even for a flat country, but not steep. So far no problem at all, but this is gradually beginning to change. Temperatures are rising, the headwinds or sidewinds are getting stronger. Ahead of me I see the long, long road which drags straight through this terribly monotonous black desert. Left and right of me cold, dreary lava rock which reflects the heat of the sun. This is how it goes on for hours. I already take great delight when I see any thriving shrub which here and there manages to hold out despite all these hard stones. "You have to be just as tough as these shrubs today, Henry, then you'll manage it!" A couple of dried out tufts of grass suddenly make me ask myself when the last rainfall must have been. Although the sky is clouded on many days, as it is today, the temperatures are between 32° and 35° in the shade. Shade, that's something that we don't have here in the desert. What I find even more difficult is the high humidity, this sauna climate.

After my moderate swimming time I still feel fine and am constantly overtaking athletes. From the tops of the hills I admire the endless chain of cyclists, it's just lovely to look at. Numerous Ironman 'marshals' on motorbikes check that the slipstream regulation is being obeyed. This means keeping 10m away from the man in front and 2m to the man on your side.

At the foot of the mountain leading to Hawi the notorious **Mumuku** wind becomes even stronger. In any case not the way it did during my first Ironman. A gradient of 5-6% and the wind is blowing sometimes head-on, sometimes from the side. This is a serious 'blow' to my average cycling time up to now and I'm a little angry. Thank God that all other competitors have this problem too. On this stretch of the journey the leading top athletes start coming back towards me. Cycling boldly and daringly, their faces all still marked by the climb, they race down the valley. Now I too look forward to that section.

This turning point in Hawaii always gives me the opportunity to keep up one of my usual habits: counting the number of athletes ahead of me. Counting how many cyclists come towards me is a source of variety on this monotonous cycle.

After a total of four hours in competition I notice my first signs of fatigue. The great euphoria of the first few hours has partially disappeared; or is it because I just couldn't get enough sleep in the last eight days? Nevertheless, I am delighted to be here doing this in Hawaii. The second time has also been an amazing experience for me so far – the tops!

I am still yearning for the turning point and am excitedly looking forward to the downhill section. But until then, it means pedalling, fighting, fighting, and pedalling. Up in this barren mountainside, however, there is no longer the monotonous grey of the desert, but left and right from the road a little grass, and even a few houses. This makes me assume that the village of Hawi must be coming up next. I pedal with even more strength now and hope that I can regenerate a bit on the way back down. Up here I see the first punctures. I hope I don't get a flat tyre. That would then cost me 6-8 minutes, and if so.....it's still not the end of the world. Every triathlete must live with this problem.

Throughout all these thought processes I keep on counting those athletes coming towards me. A seemingly endless chain of cyclists whizz in my direction at irregular intervals. "You've nearly managed this damned section," I say to myself encouragingly. The climb gradually eases. That could be, no, that must be the peak with the village of Hawi.

I suddenly sense a feeling of great relief, as if I had already finished the whole Ironman when I recognise the turning point on the horizon. "At last!" I pant. I'm happy with my performance up to now. Hopefully I didn't use up too much of my strength in the first four hours!

It's only here in Hawi that the real Ironman begins, is what I had said to myself beforehand. Is this really the case, I ask myself doubtfully. Shortly after the turning point, assistants hand me the drink and snack I had lying there since this morning. A few more

tasty bars and my energy drink are given to me as I cycle past slowly. This is how I summon up both physical and mental energy. I rejoice as I start my way back using the big chain gear and it's downhill! Yesterday, on the day before the race, I couldn't imagine doing any athletic activity in this climate. But now,.......I am able to do this after all, I realize up here. At each of the numerous aid stations, I continue taking in drinks as before. Regardless of whether I'm thirsty or not, my motto is: get it into me! Now and then I pour a bottle of water over my head and that helps for a few minutes. At mile number 70 I have managed to overcome the dreaded mountain well enough; despite all the effort I derive pleasure from the people here on this sunny island, who sporadically appear to urge us athletes on.

The many athletes now pass through the little town of Kawaihae again. The wind just keeps on blowing. However I still cannot get used to it and still find it extremely disturbing; an enemy I can fight against but a battle that I cannot win. The endless, straight road with minor, long climbs is ahead of me again. I should be at the finish in about two hours, no, at the second finish, the cycle-run transition zone. And then only another 26.2 miles, my triathlon dessert.

A great source of encouragement for me is the fact that my running times in competition are always good, i.e. better than planned. I take a banana at a few aid stations and eat them. An energy bar every hour, that was what I had planned. I do away with this plan now as I simply have enough of this sweet stuff. However I stick rigidly to my drinks. Despite this enormous amount of fluid I don't feel the need to go to the toilet. As a person who perspires strongly this doesn't surprise me much. I don't make use of the provisional toilet facilities on my way.

From mile 80 onwards everything works again for me, as I say to myself - only another - 32 miles on the bike. Only another little training session: "OK Henry, pedal, pedal, and pedal again! You wanted it this way!" Three or four miles before the airport, which lies about 7 miles out of Kailua-Kona, I recognize the turning point of the running distance. I feel at home again here. My cycling speed increases immediately. If only I were back here again, then I'd have nearly managed it all, then I'd be only thinking about getting to the finish, about finishing, then......then.......then. I already start dreaming of running through the finish. A dream I've had many times this year. How many days have I spent training for this day. Now and the hours ahead of me will show if I'm an 'Ironman'.

I think about the many good wishes I received from my fellow triathletes, my many acquaintances and friends. I've always had the feeling that these wishes came from the heart. That is why they do me a lot of good right now as it starts getting serious. The amount of confidence they had in me makes me feel confident too, and sure that I will win this challenge that I set myself.

I was often here at the airport in the last week, which is why I feel so at home now. Nevertheless, my neck and shoulder muscles are starting to play up now after five hours on the bike. I try to ease this tension by circling my arms, rolling my head and shaking my hands.

Shortly before Kailua-Kona the first professionals come running towards me with long endurance strides. Mark ALLEN and Dave SCOTT are having their duel of the century. When I look at them they give the impression as if they had neither swum 2.4 miles nor cycled for 112 miles. Totally unbelievable. Later on I heard that they finished their marathon run in 2:40 and 2:41 hours. That's faster than my best time of 2:44 hours. Naturally enough these super athletes are escorted the whole time by press and camera cars.

Then at last Kailua-Kona. Thousands of people are cheering, squealing and urging us on, as we approach them, not appearing as fresh as we were earlier. Only another 5 miles to the second transition zone after these 112 miles on the bike. The last few miles on the bike are quite difficult for me. At the same time I'm looking forward to the upcoming run. The blossoming hedges and green trees that only grow in and around Kona offer a welcome change. The air here in this little town is still, there's nothing left of the desert lava. At the same time more and more athletes come towards me, already on their marathon run. An amazing number of runners have already started walking. Then, 1 mile before the target, one last - totally exertive - climb. "Is this really necessary?" These discouraged words run through my lips. The organizers, or God above, certainly wanted to bully us today! In front of me a female triathlete keels over from her bike, she's already worn out. "How is that going to end up?" I ask myself. With incredible energy I enter the cycle finish, the euphoric commentator on the microphone announces: And here comes Henry Ash. The applause that goes out at the same time really does me good. I did it. I did it. No, I still have to do the third and final stage of my march today. I spent exactly 5:39 hours on the bike. I'm very satisfied with myself.

As in the first transition, I also take my time for this phase of the competition. More time than the professionals do. I need a good four minutes to change my jersey and my shoes.

My running time therefore already stands at four minutes when I take on the third and last part, the 26.2 mile running distance - my triathlon dessert.

After a total of 7:12 hours up to now, I do feel a bit exhausted. The climatic conditions and the 112 miles on the bike have left their mark. However, I run the first steep 500yds quite quickly. Most athletes run up here at a quick speed. "Run every mile in 8 minutes!", I force into my head at the beginning of the running distance. From the many marathons I have run I know that what is OK at mile 20 can be K.O. at mile 23. The 'marathon devil' is lurking at every corner of this run. I don't think seriously about a possible placement after seven hours out here in the lava desert. This is completely unimportant at this point. Finishing is my slogan now. It's about arriving at the finish in Kailua-Kona. I already start becoming euphoric about this, without an inkling of what is still to come. As careful as I am, I still believe I can manage a time of three hours and 30 minutes. But these miles have to be run first under the burning sun of the Pacific isles and this is quite clear to me.

At each of the aid stations, which are 1 mile apart from each other, I take a beaker filled with water and one with an electrolyte drink. I often have a slice of bread with jam with me as well. As I recognize my wife standing with several other assistants, my pace immediately speeds up. With a few funny remarks, the victory sign over my head with my right hand and the comment that I'll manage it in daylight today, I continue to run on quickly. "You're certainly brave enough today Henry!", I confirm to myself.

After about 45 minutes of running. I head out into the lava desert which is almost completely free of vegetation. Another 20 miles, a good 10 miles there and then only 10 miles back again. I've already managed 121 of my 140 miles, a pathetic 20 is all I need to do now. With the running rhythm that I've settled into, I'm constantly in the fast lane. This feels good and keeps up my motivation.

The sun slowly sets on the horizon, a picturesque view for any onlooker. As well as this, the endless coast road is filled up with running, trotting and walking triathletes. Now in the afternoon there is a light wind and hardly any drop in the temperature. From mile to mile, it gets more and more difficult to run, even for me. I comfort myself with the evidently more serious problems that other competitors from all corners of the world are having today. The same procedure at every aid station. I grab the beaker, walk

along quickly for several paces so that I can finish the entire drink where possible, and then I run on. If you can call it run. No, no, with my moderate running tempo of about approx. 8 miles per hour, that is still a slightly solid training tempo, I comfort myself. I call out some words of encouragement to many of those I have overtaken, without becoming short of breath myself.

I pass the airport. I yearn for the turning point at mile 16. "It must be soon now, it can't be much further" I keep on saying to myself. But on the seemingly endless straight road there is still no turning point in sight, I gradually begin to get impatient. Is it really after the next hill? I don't pay any more attention to milestones now. The turning point, the turning point, it almost becomes a fixed partial target for me. And then it's only another 10 miles. I like those 10 miles, only another 10 when I'm at the turn. These thoughts distract me somewhat from my legs, which are getting heavier and heavier by the minute. The climbing yards are particularly difficult.

I look at triathletes who are obviously struggling more than I am. "You'll manage it Henry, you're going to get through this Hawaii triathlon." I think again of the many good wishes of those 'suffering' with me at home.

"The turn, the turn!" I rejoice. I can see it, that builds me up a good bit. Despite all my problems, I still continue to overtake others. Shortly before the turning point, a young athlete comes towards me, tumbling along more than running. He could almost be my son. He's as white as a sheet and his deep, sunken eyes look terrible. He has obviously reached the end of his strength.. The numerous assistants will help him. I calm myself down a little. "But does it have to be like this? Is this really necessary? Is that still sport? No, you're not going to let yourself go that far," I reassure myself. There are more important things in life than finishing in an Ironman in a good time!

Luckily, my own difficulties today in my second Ironman in Hawaii are not half as dramatic as those on my first time. They are considerably milder than the hurdles that I had to overcome 4 years ago. This is certainly not only a result of my improved training condition, but of my conscious healthy eating in the last two years. Drinking Brottrunk regularly has had a positive effect on my important metabolism. From this aspect, the lack of absolute rock-bottom incidents today, which made me feel like a run-down motor four years ago, comes as a great surprise.

On the way back towards the finish I pass by the airport again for the fourth and last time. How long have I been waiting for this moment? I'll manage the remaining 7 miles, I'm completely sure of that. I still stick to my food and drink strategy. I have now drunk about two bucketfuls of fluid at this stage and have only had to pass water twice during the run as yet. The human body is a work of wonder.

Without a net top getting in the way, I can keep pouring cold water easily over my upper body. Since the turning point I have started taking a beaker of Coca-Cola along with the obligatory water and electrolyte drink. This drink which is untypical for endurance sportsmen, only serves to raise my blood sugar levels, which have hit a low. Even though my legs don't feel any lighter with it, I still maintain an almost constant running tempo as I reach the sign indicating the last three miles. Only another 3 miles and my finishing time will start with a '10'. I rejoice. Am I really going to be a whole hour faster than I was four years ago?

I'm beginning to fall in love with this cursed, but yet fascinating, 140 mile Hawaii-Ironman. I consciously savor the last three miles, not least because of the ever-growing swarm of spectators lining the Highway 19, waiting to welcome us as finishers in Kailua-Kona. My running becomes more relaxed and my strides greater. I can still manage to reach the finishing line in daylight as I had promised. During these last few miles, I positively 'fly' past a number of triathletes.

After more than 10-and-a-half hours struggle with the waves in the Pacific Ocean, with the 1 400 swimmers, the lava desert, the hills, the wind, the heat, the humidity, the 112 mile cycle and marathon, I am now floating towards the finish. The spectators are becoming more and more frenzied, indicating this long-awaited finish. Another two roads to run in Kailua-Kona, the cheering and celebrating is indescribable. "Do these people really mean me?" I ask myself. Then I turn in onto the final straight, am still able to overtake other participants. An incredible feeling. This is what drives us all to come here, I'm suddenly absolutely sure.

Among thunderous applause and cheering, I only subconsciously take in "Henry Ash - the author of many triathlon books." Celebrations within me and all around me. Fantastic, I'm at the FINISH of the Hawaii Ironman Triathlon, after 10:44 hours.

A feeling I cannot describe! Unbelievable! Dreamlike! Unbeatable!
All superlatives are valid here all at the same time!
An experience you cannot buy, even an adventure!

With an immense feeling of pride, I have the Hawaiian lei placed around my neck. I actually did manage to reach the finish in daylight. I receive the priceless Finisher T-shirt from one of the many colorfully dressed Hawaiian girls, who carry out their duties with a permanent smile. At the same time, I am led over to the massage bench and am celebrated as a finisher, which feels the same as being the overall winner in Hawaii.

After these brilliant 10 hours, 44 minutes and 21 seconds, the day is by no means over for me. As well as the very pleasant massage, a further highlight is the Grand Final. I'm not going to let this midnight spectacle pass tonight, even if I'm physically empty at the moment.

The time up to midnight flies by. After the massage, one has to set about filling up the empty carbohydrate stores. All thinkable foods possible are now available for us triathletes for this purpose.

I bump into triathletes everywhere. Everyone is talking about their experiences of the last few hours. The weatherman Kalli NOTTRODT is in his age group still right up at the front in Hawaii, and he tells of his impressions on the day. As it gets dark my friend George KROEGER comes to a very relaxed finish - this is his third finish here in a row. We still have a great laugh about our strange encounter a few days ago out in the Pacific Ocean. George was wearing the luminous red swimming trunks of his Non-Stop-Cologne club, and during my first training session at 8 in the morning I suddenly recognized him far out in the middle of the ocean. We greeted each other so heartily that we both ended up swallowing a lot of water!

The TWIN team, BARBARA and ANGELIKA, also have a great performance, landing right at the front in their age category.

With many more triathlon friends, we look for a place on the stand for the last hour of Ironman and cheer on the many triathletes that are still approaching the finish. Everyone enjoys these hours, covered in goose pimples. I could give a list of superlatives to describe this, just phenomenal!

Then it's nearly midnight. All spectators, athletes, assistants and helpers are going mad. They're all up since 4 o'clock this morning and have cheered and celebrated each individual athlete. Helpers who have flown in from the American mainland and Canada in order to take over certain duties. Athletes who have fought the whole day with the heat and the route itself, in some cases until they fell over. Sportsmen, who had to give up because

their bikes were defect, because they had overestimated themselves, because they paid too much attention to the other
competitors, because health problems set in, because ... because
... because. If they were close to tears a minute ago, they are now
captured by the incredible euphoria all around. The brilliant man
at the microphone - now almost hoarse - who with great zest has
made this Ironman an experience for the spectators as well since 6
o'clock this morning, interupts the reggae music for a moment, to
which hundreds are already dancing, and calls out into the night
"Hey you out there! Whoever you are - you've got two minutes to
the time limit. Hurry up before the curtain falls." Everyone shouts
along together "Come on, you'll manage it, come on, come on."
One more minute. The crowds are running. The speaker interrupts
the music that drowns out anything else. "I can see a runner, a
runner is coming. Help him. My friends, help him." The people
bawl and cheer into the night. You can hardly hear the roar of the
ocean. Another 30 seconds. The female runner appears at the end
of the stand. Nobody is sitting on their seats anymore. 20 seconds,
a sprint. The Japanese woman is struggling and cheering at the
same time. Another 10 seconds. She then races across the finishing line. The public goes completely crazy. The last Ironman in
this year's competition. Deadline!

We all have hot and cold running down our backs. Pity for all
those who are still out on the marathon even after 17 hours and
who'll be then picked up by street vans.

This is what awaits every athlete who takes on the calculable
Ironman adventure. An adventure which you still cannot buy no
matter how much you've got in your wallet. You just have to do it
yourself, with the help of willpower and with the mental and
physical strength you have worked up by yourself.

Be it in Hawaii, in Austria, in Switzerland, in Florida, in
Germany, in Canada, in Lanzarote, Malaysia, or anywhere else,
you have the opportunity to experience this adventure all round
the world.

The previous day was an exhausting, adventurous experience. The night was short and all your limbs are now asking for a little exercise. Careful stretching exercises are on the agenda. Breakfast cannot be sumptuous enough. After all you have earned it. Now it's time for savoring the success, innerly and outerly. Every finisher may be proud of his successful performance, even if it did not work out perfectly here and there. Many athletes have problems with their finishing times. Is that really necessary? Is it not the deep and gripping experience that one gathered over the 140 miles that are more valuable than a mere time result?

Of course the fnishing time achieved is one factor of success, but not the only one thank God, and definitely not the most important one.

Maybe it's possible to take a short, very gentle swim when it's warm, maybe a little cycle will do you good or even a comfortable little run.

There are plenty of topics for conversation today at the prize-giving or at the triathlon exhibition, with the assistants, with friends and acquaintances. Everyone is allowed to enjoy heroic status for himself today.

The noble triathlon title "Ironman" is the perfect name for anyone who, with his own muscular strength, succeeded in swimming 2.4 miles, cycling 112 miles and then running 26.2 to finish off.

Any athlete who has successfully tackled this three-course meal, is a real Ironman and can already start dreaming today of the next Ironman competition.

What was the way there again?
DREAM - GOAL - IRONMAN

CHAPTER 12

Regeneration

The Basis for Performance-oriented Training

The amount of time that passes between two training sessions is extremely important for an endurance sportsman. In this phase not only our body, but also our mind and soul, recover from the last training. If this break is too short, this inevitably leads to overtraining. Breaks that are too long, however, lead to a drop in performance. Neither of these is beneficial to a performance-oriented sportsman. The trick behind balanced triathlon training is finding out the right relationship between sporting exertion and recovery.

There are often great differences in the measures one can go to in order to get back to one's performance capacity level. Some measures must be heeded, others can be taken into account.

Regeneration after a Training Session

Just as it is with all sporting achievements - where some athletes are talented and others not so - the reasons for this have certainly something to do with genetics - it's the same with regeneration. There are athletes who regenerate quickly and those who need a bit longer for regeneration.

Nevertheless, there are some important basis principles, which, when heeded, can reduce recovery time. Included here are a number of various measures.

As these are particularly important for Masters, they are illustrated in detail below. Every athlete now has the opportunity to choose those measures which bring him the best possible benefit.

Master who regenerate quickly are able to take up their normal training quota earlier again. They train more effectively and have a higher performance level than those who require a longer break following an exertive training session.

The blood circulation in the tired and exhausted muscles is worse than normal because of the formation of lactic acid and urea. Light to medium activities after sporting exertion enhance the oxygen supply and thus also the blood circulation in the tired muscles. For these reasons **active** regeneration is more effective than passive regeneration, i.e. total rest.

Active Regenerative Measures

These include:

Cool-Off

For a triathlete this means finishing off with relaxed cycling for 30 minutes or relaxed swimming for 500yds followed by several stretching exercises.

Dry Training Clothing

Dry training clothing is one of the first things to think about. One must avoid chilling and catching a cold as a result. Although I know this myself, I have often forgot my own rules and ended up catching a cold for 2-3 days, because I hung about chatting.

Food And Fluid Intake

Our water and electrolyte balance is distorted through loss of sweat. The metabolic by-products lactic acid and urea must be broken down as soon as possible. One can then shorten this natural period of recovery with suitable drinks.

Sufficient sleep

The amount of sleep required differs from person to person, ranging from a minimum of 5 hours to a maximum of 10 hours. Endurance athletes tend to have a deeper sleep than those who don't carry out sport. Having said this, hard training late in the evening can cause sleeping problems. As well as this, such problems often can be the first sign of overtraining.

Stretching

Regular stretching exercises after training, and particularly after competition, improves one's sense of well-being, body feeling and helps to quicken up the regeneration process. Stretching exercises help to cut down muscular tension and improve the flexibility of our joints.

Massage

What is seen as a luxury among hobby sportsmen is for numerous competitive athletes an essential part of training - massage. The physical and mental benefits lsted below go to show the importance of this regenerative measure.

▲ Joints, tendons and ligament are brought to life.

▲ Any muscular tension is loosened up.

▲ Mental tension or nervosity can be reduced.

▲ Metabolism is improved.

Relaxation Baths

After long training sesssions one just has to enjoy a relaxing bath. In the first three hours after exertion, they play a significant role in improving blood circulation to the muscles.

Sauna, Jacuzzi

Regular visits to the sauna help regeneration to a considerable extent. One should stop going to the sauna two days before competition. After training or competition one should cut these visits down to one or two. The great amount of body fluid lost after a sauna should be compensated for by drinks of mineral content. Alcohol has an effect here as it hinders the building-up processes which take place during regeneration.

Electrical Muscular Stimulation (EMS)

Electrical muscular stimulation devices are being used more and more often, particularly after competitions or hard training sessions. The special regeneration programs e.g. by COMPEX-SPORT take about 25 minutes and enable the removal of lactate, an improvement in blood circulation and thus the quicker renewal of muscular performance. The muscles are not contracted here, but rather are subject to a series of vibrations.

Concentrationg On Other Matters Apart From Sport

Walks, wandering tours, cycling trips with the family, visits to

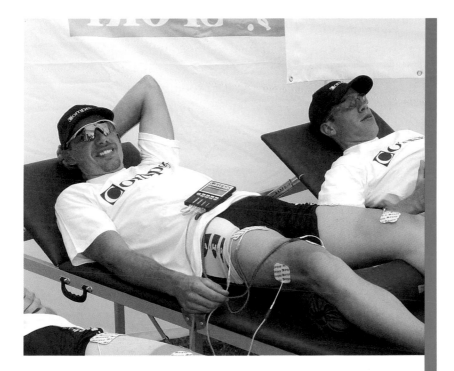

adventure swimming pools, reading, handicrafts, doing things with other family members, DIY, all these activities can (but don't have) to help the process of regeneration.

As well as this, a short holiday and the acknowledgement of the fact that there are other things in life than merely swimming, cycling, running, exercises and strength training, do a great lot for one's physical and particularly one's mental regeneration

Regeneration within a Training Week

Even within a hard week of training, regenerative measures must not be neglected. Let me comment on the term 'hard'. What I mean here is a training week that involves a lot of exertion, and this is often referred to as hard in sporting circles. Apart from this the term 'hard' is not really appropriate in Master sports. Life can be hard, but not the fun-oriented sport that we chose ourselves.

For ambitious competitive athletes, the days for training within a week can be allocated as follows:

▲ Two days of training in a row: (Tues./Wed:)
▲ One day for regeneration (Thurs.)
▲ Three days of training in a row (Fri./ Sat./ Sun.)
    i.e. with a rhythm of 2:1:3:1.

Needless to say, the various active regenerative measures mentioned above must be carried out also within a training week.

Regeneration within a Training Month

Apart from the normal training weeks (N) and regeneration weeks (R), top-class athletes also have hard weeks of training in the competition period. For the reasons already mentioned, Masters ought to go without these hard weeks of training. The following training rhythm within a month can be recommended for younger Masters.

▲ Normal training week (N)
▲ Normal training week (N)
▲ Normal training week (N)
▲ Regeneration week (R),
    i.e. N/N/N/R, N/N/N/R, etc.

Better for older Masters is:
▲ Normal training week (N)
▲ Normal training week (N)
▲ Regeneration week (R)
    i.e. N/N/R, N/N/R, etc.

Training rhythm naturally varies according to one's level of performance, age, preparation period, competition period, personal circumstances among others.

Have a look at the concrete training recommendations to see just what these training weeks look like in compliance with the individual Masters' demands.

The general rule for the regeneration weeks: drastically reduce training volume and intensity.

Regeneration after a Competition

As soon as you have crossed the finish line, you ought to start carrying out a regeneration program. Having already explained the various measures to be taken, I can now recommend the following order to do them in:

1. A short breather, take electrolyte drinks.
2. Put on dry training clothing.
3. Stretching exercises.
4. 5-10 minutes cool-off trot, or cool-off swim for 500yds.
5. Take a shower.
6. Perhaps massage.
7. Plenty of electrolyte drinks.
8. Food that is rich in carbohydrates.
9. Perhaps a hot bath.
10. Perhaps electrical muscular stimulation.

"After competition is before a competition" is the motto here. The points already discussed serve to loosen up the exhausted muscles, which in turn promote the breakdown of metabolic waste. Electrolyte drinks and foods rich in carbohydrates are of significant importance for fast and effective regeneration. Apart from this, the same principles regarding regenerative measures after training hold here too.

The days directly after a competition are for training sessions at very low levels of intensity only. Priority is to be given to swimming and cycling here, as these forms of sport involve less strain on the body. The least amount of time for regeneration is required with swimming. This is due to the relatively short muscular exertion here.

After hard, exerting competitions regeneration does not just take a few days. It can often take several weeks. Only then should one begin with normal training again. There is no set formula regarding the length of time needed for regeneration. Among other things, it depends on length of competition, number of years in training, training state, genetic factors.

Approximate Regeneration Times for Masters

Distance	Newcomers	Advanced
10km run	1-2 weeks	1 week
Marathon	4 weeks	2 weeks
Triathlon Middle Distance	3 weeks	2 weeks
Ironman Distance	4 weeks	3 weeks

An athlete who does not allow his mind and body enough time for regeneration and then increases his training too quickly and takes part in too many competitions, will sooner or later be confronted with the problem of 'overtraining'.

CHAPTER 13

Overtraining

Those Athletes who Overdo Things

When, instead of the anticipated improvement in one's performance, one notices a definite deterioration despite being in good health in training, this is a clear symptom of overtraining. A Master who carries out triathlon from a very performance-oriented perspective ought to get to grips with the risk of being overtrained.

Overtraining can be diagnosed in a medical check-up by measuring the concentration of urea in the blood. If the rate is over 50 the athlete is overtrained. Which Masters are in danger here?

Those athletes who

▲ do not have a sufficient basis for their intensive training, i.e. have neglected basic endurance training.

▲ take their sport too 'seriously'.

▲ do not take private and working factors into account when organizing training, i.e. ignore their personal circumstances.

▲ train at intensities that are too high.

▲ do not allow themselves sufficient regeneration time.

▲ take part in too many competitions.

Even without a medical examination, it is possible to recognize when one is overtrained through the following symptoms:

▲ Indifference, no interest in training

▲ Frequent occurrence of colds, fever

▲ Drop in performance despite an increase in training

▲ Querying one's training

▲ Inability to relax

▲ Rise in rest heart rate of 10-15 beats

▲ Sweating at night, diarrhoea, constipation

▲ Lack of strength in training

▲ Problems getting to sleep

▲ Lack of concentration, depression

▲ Restless sleep at night

▲ Aches in muscles and joints

▲ Lack of appetite, loss in weight

What measures can I take in order to combat this state of overtraining successfully?

What do I do to avoid overtraining in the first place?

The points below, listed in random order, are worth considering here. I can recommend you to do as follows:

▲ Plan more days of rest and stick to them.
▲ Only carry out regenerative training i.e. at lower levels of intensity 50-60%.
▲ Put the principle "Sport is meant to be fun" actually into practice.
▲ Join a training group which train more calmly.
▲ Give yourself a change of surroundings, i.e. holiday or long weekend.
▲ Abstain from alcohol and nicotine.
▲ Clearly reduce training volume in the competition period.
▲ Only take part in competitions after many months of preparation, with training at low to medium intensity.
▲ By all means keep up the regeneration weeks after competitions.
▲ Keep a training diary in order to be able to check and compare.
▲ Make sure your transitional period (major regeneration) is long enough.
▲ Reduce the number of competitions per year considerably.
▲ Get enough sleep.
▲ Have variety in your training. Train within a group more often.
▲ Don't take every triathlon 'deadly seriously'. There are more important things in life than just swimming, cycling and running.
▲ Do not necessarily take part in every competition with 100% effort. 85-90% may also be enough for you to have fun.
▲ You're better postponing a training session than sticking to your program with grim determination.
▲ Only a slow increase in training load may occur following injuries.

Whoever takes some of these measures to heart, and reminds himself again and again that sport serves to improve one's health, and not the other way round, will be able to take up his sporting activities again after a while with more fun and enjoyment. Just how long this state of overtraining remains, with all its negative consequences - whether weeks or months - depends entirely upon yourself.

If you identify the problem of overtraining relatively early, on then you also have a good chance of regenerating again pretty quickly. However, if you let yourself get into this mess for weeks and months i.e. into the state of overtraining, and are not willing to admit this either for a long time, this may cost you an entire season. It's often the case that the grim and determined athletes blame others for their unexpected weak competition performance, their training group, the weather, the high workload, the family, the slow training etc etc.

It's generally easier to put the blame on others; the more honest way, and certainly the way that will lead to success again, is to start working on oneself first and analyze oneself critically with the points mentioned earlier. A further tip here, ask an experienced sports friend to help you get to the root of your state of overtraining. One has to identify the cause first before being able to start with the appropriate cure.

CHAPTER 14

Triathlon and Nutrition

In Chapter 12 of 'Lifelong Success - Triathlon: Training For Masters" I have already looked in great detail at the basic aspects of a triathlete's diet as well as any questions specifically for training and competition. For this reason I only point out some brief tips on this matter below:

▲ Running with a completely empty bladder can cause damage to the bladder's mucous membrane. The outcome of this is red urine after the competition.

▲ Set up a food plan before the competition.

▲ Take in 150-200ml every 15-20 minutes (easy to remember!), The body can take in up to 800ml in an hour.

▲ 1.5-2 miles before steep uphill sections, take a good large gulp of fluid.

▲ The right sports drink provides a balanced mix of minerals and vitamins, as minerals and water-soluble vitamins are lost through sweating.

▲ Electrolytes of particular importance are: magnesium and calcium (for effective musular function, prevents cramps).

▲ Potassium and sodium are important for the body's water balance.

▲ Despite water intake, it is still possible for the body to become dehydrated when this water contains no sodium.

▲ Five minutes before the start take a drink of 300-500ml.

COCA-COLA in competition?

Coke is low in electrolytes. With 460 kcal/l it does contain a lot of energy, however only in the form of simple sugars, which raise one's blood sugar level dramatically. This in turn causes the pancreas to distribute an increased amount of insulin. At the same time the liver is hindered from giving off glucose. The glucose already supplied is used up very quickly, however new supplies from the liver are too low. As a result blood sugar levels drop again, sometimes even to below original levels, a state of exhaustion sets in.

So, either keep on working on new glucose supplies (every 10-15 minutes) or better, take a drink containing more long-chained carbohydrates. They enter the blood more slowly and keep insulin levels relatively constant.

The same principle should also hold for solid foods.

Thus the important things are:
1. Test out drinks in training to see if you can tolerate them.
2. Find out what drinks will be handed out at the official catering stands.
3. Have your own drinks with you where necessary.
4. Never take ice-cold drinks.

CHAPTER 15

Triathlon Highlights

Ironman Events around the World

You can find the latest results, all information regarding the Hawaii Ironman and the qualifying competitions at:

www.ironmanlive.com.

The dates for the next Ironman in Hawaii are:

October 23, 2004
October 15, 2005

Ironman Triathlon World Championship, Event date: October
There are currently 24 Ironman events in which it is possible to qualify for the Ironman World Championship in Hawaii within one's individual age category.

These are:
Ironman Langkawi Malaysia Triathlon, Event date: February
Ironman New Zealand Triathlon, Event date: March
Ralphs Ironman California Triathlon, Event date: April
Ironman Australia Triathlon, Event date: April
Half IM St. Croix, Event date: May
Lanzarote Canarias Ironman Triathlon, Event date: May
Ironman Japan, Event date: May
Ironman Brazil Triathlon, Event date: May
Keauhou-Kona Triathlon, Event date: May
Utah Half Ironman Triathlon, Event date: May
Blackwater EagleMan Triathlon, Event date: June
Ironman France Triathlon, Event date: June
Buffalo Springs Lake Triathlon, Event date: June
Ironman USA Coeur d'Alene Triathlon, Event date: June
Ironman Austria Triathlon, Event date: July
Ironman Germany Triathlon, Event date: July
Ironman Switzerland Triathlon, Event date: July
Ironman Lake Placid, Event date: July
Half Vineman Triathlon, Event date: August
Ironman Canada Triathlon, Event date: August
Ironman Korea Triathlon, Event date: August
Half Ironman UK, Event date: September
Ironman Wisconsin Triathlon, Event date: September
Janus Ironman Florida Triathlon, Event date: November

The Fascination of the Ironman Hawaii Triathlon

What's behind it all when triathletes, supervisors, spectators and others give statements on the Ironman Hawaii like:

▲ Ironman, more than a race!

▲ Hawaii is 'Wimbledon for triathletes!'

▲ Ironman - the epitome of triathlon!

▲ Ironman, the ultimate challenge!

▲ Ironman is like hot and cold, like black and white, or good and bad together. Good because it is so intensive, just as in a big family, bad because you're captured in it and cannot get out.

With all these comments, one thing becomes very clear: this Hawaii Ironman must possess something special, mystical and distinctive for triathletes.

Below I will try to explain the very secrets of the Ironman-Hawaii triathlon, to point out, visualize or simply make the spirit of the Hawaii Ironman triathlon understandable for you all, so as to give you an impression as to why the Ironman is something magical and gigantic.

The Ironman on the paradise island of Hawaii is the crowning experience for almost every triathlete. This mother of all competitions with its distinctive flair, its extraordinary climatic conditions, its perfect organization and its abundance of incredibly friendly helpers and spectators, has a magical effect on athletes all over the world.

The decision to present triathlon as an Olympic sport in 2000 gave new impulses to this combination sport. Media interest in triathlon has risen considerably both due to the performance highlights such as Hawaii and the more than twenty Ironman events worldwide, but also due to a study of 50 different forms of sport, carried out by the University of Vienna which caused a sensation. This study certified triathlon as being a sport of the future because of its top health aspects, low injury factor and environmental friendliness, and gave it the top placement in the process.

After the introduction of the official international world championships, there were voices who already proclaimed a dying end for triathlon in Hawaii. Others were of the opinion that triathlon would die off after a number of years and that the athletes would be fed up with always the same place, the same conditions... and the same winners? From a pure theoretical perspective, this could indeed be possible and this has proved to be the case in many other matters. Anything involving constant repetition is inevitably going to be out at some stage.

However, all these theories do not hold for the Hawaii Ironman one little bit. What occurs in Hawaii is the epitome of triathlon. Nowhere else in the world is there such a fascinating atmosphere surrounding a triathlon competition as in Big Island, Hawaii; neither for the athletes, nor for the spectators.

The allegedly hardest competition in the world, the certainly most turbulent swimming miles in the world, the hottest cycling route, the most extreme marathon - the sporting superlative, has a magical attraction on all those for whom triathlon has become more than just sport. Passion, fascination, the trip for every athlete.

What once was a flashy idea of a frustrated hobby sportsman has, within only a few years, turned into a sport that fills millions of people with enthusiasm and in the meantime is carried out by millions of athletes around the world. Triathlon just keeps on winning more and more fans.

Triathlon has become a trend sport

This briefly described Hawaii phenomenon is no longer just a passing craze, but rather a real situation that has now held for 25 years, becoming even stronger, even more intensive, even more challenging from year to year.

Over the last 20 years I can confirm personally that even after completing 30 Hawaii distances throughout the world, after managing a double Hawaii-distance, and after running in 80 marathons, there is NOTHING TO EQUAL THIS. The Hawaii triathlon is simply the non plus ultra for endurance athletes, the kings of endurance. I too definitely experience withdrawal symptoms after several years without doing the Ironman Hawaii. These can be seen in the fact that my creativity is really under strain - to look for realistic possibilities to be able to once again include Hawaii in my personal plans. The withdrawal symptoms really come to light when the Ironman in Hawaii is in full swing. It is impossible to even think about sleeping as not only my thoughts are with the 1 500 triathletes in Hawaii but rather my arms and legs would do anything to swim, cycle and run along too.

The Hawaii Triathlon is the ultimate challenge for all triathletes. Combined with the magical landscape of the South Sea islands, all superlatives are allowed here, and for this reason it is quite difficult to describe this in words.

At this point I would like to list a collection of quotes made by several triathletes, supervisors, commentators, spectators and escorts over the last years, which help to describe the fascination that is the Hawaii Ironman. Furthermore, these statements along with conversation notes, comments made at congresses and at discussions of the Hawaii triathlon or the numerous qualifying competitions, should all help to understand the background.

▲ Big Island of all places, the biggest and the hottest of the Hawaii islands, is the venue for the Ironman Triathlon World Championship with its endless 3,800m swimming distance in the sea, 112 miles of cycling and a marathon run of 26.2 miles.

▲ You don't necessarily have to be a Hawaii finisher to be spellbound by Ironman. Every non-triathlete is impressed by the distances alone as well as the climatic conditions of Hawaii. The conquest against one's weaker self is not the only thing that has made Ironman become the most significant triathlon in the world.

▲ Even with Olympic Games and World Championships the mythos of Hawaii will continue to exist.

▲ The Hawaii triathlon, known as the extreme non-stop endurance test, also provides us with the opportunity to completely challenge ourselves mentally with a combination of the most popular endurance sports of swimming, cycling and swimming.

▲ When 'Ironman Fever' breaks out in Kona on the Big Island, we're not just talking about a mild rise in temperature here, but rather a full hot flush, up to a state of delirium! Ironman and Triathlon are magic words which bring a sparkle to every native's eyes. Triathlon is so incredibly popular, that it's almost too much. An Ironman menu in every restaurant, Ironman cocktail at the bar, Ironman T-shirts over chest muscles of iron and pot bellies, Ironman sundaes, Ironman pizzas all at steep Ironman prices.

▲ Anyone wishing to experience triathlon can do so to a sheer extreme in Kailua-Kona. There's hardly any other better place for this.

▲ An Ironman or Ironwoman who has ever ploughed their way through the Pacific, cycles and runs across the fields of lava, has already come down with Kona-Fever, and will never lose this again either. And anyone who has ever dreamed of roaming around the 'Sandwich Islands' should just arrange this in such a way that on Race Day he is at the finish in the evening, long after the sun has set. There really is nothing in the world that can compare with the atmosphere, enthusiasm and sporting fun that exists here.

▲ Hawaii is the ultimate challenge for the human body. To win in Hawaii means more than an Olympic victory.

▲ It's for this race that I carry out triathlon. That says everything about its meaning for me!

▲ On the Short distance one is mainly competing against others, in Hawaii and on the Long distance one is competing against oneself alone.

▲ Despite or maybe because of the Olympic Games, the magical attraction of Ironman is just as strong as ever; the term Ironman-Hawaii still implies the non plus ultra competition for endurance sportsmen. This race unites the mythos of any other imaginable sporting highlights in one, such as:

• the Wimbledon Tournament for tennis players

• the Tour de France for cyclists

• the Admiral's Cup for sailing sportsmen

• simply the dream, the crowning experience, the ultimate peak in triathlon.

Finally we must ask: "What part of the swimming, cycling and running ironman is actually made of 'iron' ?

▲ The heart? Hardly, considering the endurance training that is necessary.

▲ The lung? With a competition that goes on for 8-17 hours, this would be impossible.

▲ The muscles? These are under continuous strain and must therefore be the exact opposite of iron and static, i.e. elastic and flexible.

The only thing that's left over here is a **will of iron**, which is necessary for reaching the finish after 140 swimming, cycling and running miles despite all the difficulties that may occur.

This Ironman Hawaii *spirit*, the fascination behind this Hawaii triathlon is something that you just have to experience, whether as a triathlete, assistant, official, trainer, reporter, family member or simply as a tourist, so as to be able to understand the real value of this impressive adventure.

I hope that I was able to give you a brief insight into all this in Chapter 11 "The Day Has finally Come."

For all those who are not able to get to Hawaii for particular reasons (sporting, financial, work, family), there is of course still the possibility of finishing in one of the bigger triathlon events worldwide and fullfilling one's Ironman dream in this way. However it is just as possible to experience the Hawaii feeling elsewhere in the world, be it in Austria, Germany, Switzerland, Lanzarote to mention but a few.

CHAPTER 16

Power Thinking

For Masters

By Dr. Barbara Warren, San Diego

For general mental strength

Train your brain. Power thinking is a habit of thought patterns. Keep your thinking on track by not permitting negative feelings to slip into your mind. Power thinking is target-directed, intentional, premeditated, and planned. Your brain is a chemical powerhouse that can take you farther than you ever imagined if you allow it to play its part. By means of speed and force your thoughts criss-cross your brain with spectacular electrical flashes. Thinking happens so fast that you often cannot hear it but you feel the effect in your emotions and therefore certain behaviors will follow. Every one of your thoughts influences cells in your body. When your emotions are uplifted you feel motivated, productive, and creative. Therefore you have a higher psychological advantage from which to view your challenges and obstacles. Power thinking is necessary for specific intense training, and racing.

1. Train your emotions not to distract you from your situation. Learn to be OK in spite of what is happening inside and outside of you.

2. Train your thinking to be specific and intense. Visualize a race or a training workout, feel the environment, and allow your self to be at your best. Do not talk with 'should" and 'have to' but convert these words into 'want to' and 'allow to'.

3. Train your brain to monitor your emotions. Use your rational thinking mode in contrast to an emotional mode that can derail you from your purpose.

4. Train your thinking for fast, efficient solutions, and decisions.

Feed your mind with brain foods

Brain foods must be energizing. Don't only eat a high-carbohydrate meal before a competition or an important training session. It makes your thinking dull.

Protein stimulates, while animal fats slow down the brain function.

Alcohol is a depressant and should be avoided if you want perfect focus and concentration.

Brain foods:

Shellfish sardines, herring, salmon, tuna beets, carrots, celery barley, brown rice, oats, lean beef, dried sprouted beans, nuts and seeds, dark-green and orange fruits, and vegetables, grapes, pears, apples, basil, ginger, licorice, rosemary, wheat germ, brewer's yeast and lecithin.

Connected Thinking

For fast and short training sessions and competitions

Connect your thinking to the present and don't allow yourself to sway into the past or future. Be in touch with your body's need and draw on your mental power for the best strategies possible. Use your narrow, internal focus to be proficient and dynamic. Connected thinking means to be centered and focused at every moments. The mind is so vibrant that it cannot stay connected consistently for more than a short period and then it will break off into a variety of thoughts that will distract from speed.

Your connected state of mind interprets information about how your body and intellect respond, like a pilot that reads the instrument panel. All the critical information is at your hands and your brain. It shows you how much longer you can endure, how much attention span you have left, and how to optimize your mind's energy to reach your best. Connected thinking is based on experience, which in turn gives you the data for the instrument panel. This information can also flash warning signals that clarify how much more you can or cannot do.

Train your mind to be alert to every warning sign of your body. Connect to the situation, to your body, and to your circumstances. Once you regroup you want to use Power thinking to be in control of the overall circumstances.

You want to deliver a faultless competition. You can endure the pain because you know there is an end to it. For the moments that you are "on" you need to be completely connected to your movements and your breathing. As long as you stay connected to the present with all your obvious needs, you will succeed.

Disconnected Thinking

For long endurance triathlons and workouts

On the other side of the spectrum we have the disconnected state of mind that is an energy-saving technique. This category of thinking can definitely expel some pain, fatigue, stress, and frustration, thus helping stamina. Disconnection is an endurance attention strategy. Picture a jogger with no real concern for speed that listens to music in order to block out discomfort and monotony. Your want to become as disconnected from what you are doing as possible, so that you won't feel the frustration that takes place by enduring many hours of physical activity. You only can do this in a race that is long and does not involve all out speed.

You engage in a stream of conscious thoughts, drifting into the past or future, into daydreaming, or any other distractions. If you are on your morning run, you might check out the scenery, give that talk that your boss expects from you, and see you future unravel or solve your daily problems.

Train yourself to disconnect from the adversities that you feel in your body, and from the frustration that you feel in your soul. You know very well the language of pain. You have been a Master in overcoming your adversities. They still will exist but you can program your mind to be distracted and you will be able to go much longer with greater efficiency.

As an example you can think of your favorite sceneries from childhood or you can open a fantasy curtain in front of you bike or on the run and make up a story with soft music, tamed animals, and many friends. At times your might sing a tune, listen to nature or dwell on building castles in the air. Disconnect your thinking by taking your mind and emotions into a wonderful, pleasant location.

Fragmented Thinking

For medium and long races

A fragmented mode of thinking wants complete concentration and focus, which will alternate with thoughts that take you away from the present struggle. You use your power thinking as a general full-blown energy discharge, which you interlink with connected and disconnected thinking. As you keep moving in a race you will unconsciously slip in and out of these different forms. For some time you will fully concentrate and focus, and next you go off into fantasyland allowing anything that is pleasant to distract your mind.

Subsequently your thinking will break up into three different ways, making way for a fourth mode called fragmentation. At times you need to connect to the present, checking the needs of your body, at other moments you want to disconnect from the pain, and further more you need a good share of mental power to keep your rational thinking on track. Specific triathlons and training conditions require the number one, two, or the third thinking mode, or all of them in one race. Have the awareness of the different modes first, and second separate one thinking mode from the others. Use the kind of thoughts that best fits the nature of your races and workouts.

Peter, 54 years old, would not be able not win if he did not use his thoughts in a precise manner. He never leaves his Power thinking at home, which he uses with control to stay on track of his workouts. When out on a very long, slow day he wants to kill time or distract from any pain by slipping into the Disconnected mode. When Peter participates in a short triathlon race he uses Connected thinking with complete focus and total concentration.

Margie is an old time triathlete who likes the Ironman distance. She has never been fast but knows how to Disconnect into la-la land for many hours at a time. For her this is the only way to go through the many hours required for the finish.

Greg has never been a very patient athlete. Many times his emotions talked so loud that he had to give up in some of his most important competitions. Greg learned not to listen to his distracting feelings. At the same time he became skilled in switching his thinking modes, which helped him to be busy at all times. Rapidly he found out that he could endure even long distances because he filled his mind with the appropriate switching of thoughts. Soon he turned into a winner.

Appendix

Tables

In order to be able to check and regulate one's training it is important to actually know one's maximum heart rate for running and cycling. Masters, enjoying good health, should not just rely on the rough formula 220 minus age for men and 226 minus age for women, but should check these values according to those methods I've looked at before at least twice a year. A good idea is during the preparation period and at the beginning of the competition period. This means for me the months February/March and June/July.

With the help of these simple values which are easy to find out, it is possible to divide up training into six stages or frequency ranges. According to age, training period, future competitions and personal circumstances, one can combine the different intensities. More concrete detailed suggestions can be found in the training recommendations.

The Six Stages of Heart Rate for different Training Loads

Step	Description of training	Running training % of max. pulse rate	Cycling training % of max. pulse rate	Form of training	Running training e.g. max. pulse 173	Cycling training e.g. max. pulse 168
1	**Easy going, refreshing** Regeneration	60-70	55-65	Fat-burning Basic endurance	104-121	93-109
2	**Calm** training	70-75	65-70	Basic endurance	121-130	109-118
3	**Easy** training	75	70	Basic endurance	130	118
4	**Brisk** training	75-80	70-75	Endurance training	130-138	118-126
5	**Very fast** training (quick)	80-85	75-80	Speed endurance training	138-147	126-134
6	**Hard** training	85-90	80-85	Tempo continuous run/Tempo cycle	147-156	134-143

The two columns on the far right enable us to conclude the following simple rule:

▲ At the same level of training intensity, the heart rate for cycling is 10% lower than for running!

An athlete who begins with endurance training must therefore train at different levels to those levels at which performance-oriented athletes train. Whereas Steps 1-2 are very important for beginners, the main proportion of training for advanced and performance-oriented Masters occurs in Steps 1-5.

Explanation of the six stages of heart rate can be found in the Chapters 4 and 5.

Heart Rate For Swimming, Cycling and Running Training

One must, however, pay attention to the fact that maximum heart rates are different for each discipline. It's helpful to check these after the first half of the preparation period and during the competition period.

My Individual Maximum Heart Rates		
Date	e.g. 03.03.05	e.g. 06.30.05
Max. Pulse Swimming	155	
Max. Pulse Cycling	168	
Max. Pulse Running	175	

You can use this example to record your own comparisons.

100%	95%	90%	85%	80%	75%	70%	65%	60%
190	181	171	162	152	143	133	124	114
188	179	169	60	150	141	132	122	113
186	177	167	158	149	140	130	121	112
184	175	166	156	147	138	129	119	110
182	173	164	155	146	136	127	118	109
180	171	162	153	144	135	126	117	108
178	169	160	151	142	134	125	116	107
176	167	158	150	141	132	123	115	106
174	165	157	148	139	130	122	113	104
172	163	155	146	138	129	120	112	103
170	162	153	144	136	127	119	110	102
168	160	151	142	134	126	118	109	101
166	158	149	141	133	124	116	108	100
164	156	148	140	131	123	115	107	98
162	154	146	138	130	122	113	105	97
160	152	144	136	128	120	112	104	96
158	150	142	134	126	118	111	103	95

156	148	140	132	125	117	109	102	94
154	146	139	131	123	116	108	100	92
152	144	137	130	122	114	106	98	91
150	143	135	128	120	112	105	97	90
148	141	133	126	118	111	104	96	89
146	139	131	124	117	110	102	95	88
144	137	129	122	115	108	101	94	86
142	135	127	120	113	107	99	92	85
140	133	126	119	112	105	98	91	84
138	131	124	117	110	104	97	90	83

Photo Credits

Title Photo: getty images

Inside Photos:
L. Amarell: p. 109
H. Ash: p. 72, 93, 112, 129, 136, 187, 208
Bakke-Svensson/WTC: p. 27, 35, 69, 107, 190, 198, 212, 223, 227, 228, 231
R. Bistricky: p. 111
Compex: p. 219
getty images: p. viii
L. Guillou: p. 203
Ironman Austria Fototeam/Thorsten Frahm: p. iii, v, xi, xvii, 3, 6, 9, 10, 19, 25, 42, 45, 53, 78, 97, 139, 140, 181, 189, 193, 215, 239, 245
K. H. Koch: p. 16
G. Schmidt: p. 81
B. Warren: p. xiii, 48

Cover Design: Birgit Engelen

Anything ...

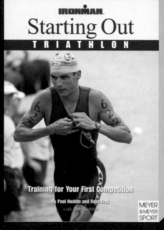

Ironman Edition
Triathlon
– Starting out
Training for Your First Competition

Here's the best book on the market to get you to the starting line. Roch Frey and Paul Huddle are the two most respected names in multi sport coaching. They cover all the bases in the first book of the Ironman Training Series. Besides running, cycling and swimming, you'll find information on everything from weight training to flexibility to nutrition. Don't sit on the sidelines any longer. With Roch and Paul at your side, anyone and everyone can do a triathlon.

160 pages
Full-colour print
81 photos, 16 tables
Paperback, 5 3/4" x 8 1/4"
ISBN: 1-84126-101-7
£ 12.95 UK / $ 17.95 US
$ 25.95 CDN / € 16.90

IRONMAN

MEYER
& MEYER
SPORT

MEYER & MEYER Sport | sales@m-m-spotrs.com | rn-m-sports.com

is Possible

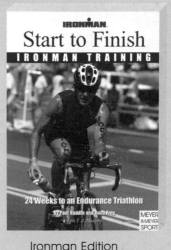

Ironman Edition
Start to Finish
Ironman Training:
24 Weeks to an Endurance Triathlon

Okay, you've finished your first short distance triathlon. Now it's time to up the ante and go further and faster. Paul and Roch are up to the challenge. Longer workouts, balancing work, family and training, adding speed work, recovery and the mental game are all essential when you decide to move up to the Olympic and then half Ironman distance. No one has more training or racing experience than Roch and Paul. They will get you to your target race healthy, happy and ready for more. Guaranteed.

176 pages
Full-colour print
Many colour photos
Paperback, 5^3/4" x 8^1/4"
ISBN: 1-84126-102-5
£ 12.95 UK / $ 17.95 US
$ 25.95 CDN / € 16.90

MEYER & MEYER Sport | sales@m-m-spotrs.com | m-m-sports.com

MEYER & MEYER SPORT

25 Legendary Years

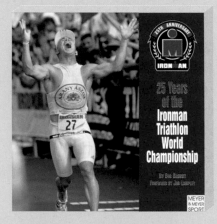

Bob Babbitt

25 YEARS OF THE IRONMAN TRIATHLON WORLD CHAMPIONSHIP

CONTENTS

Ironman Hall of Fame Inductee Bob Babbitt and some of the world's best photographers lovingly share images and stories from what many consider the Toughest Day in Sport, the Ironman. With a foreword from legendary sportscaster Jim Lampley and an introduction from Ironman creator Commander John Collins, this beautiful book chronicles an event that started out with 15 crazy entrants in 1978 and now, 25 years later, is considered the ultimate goal for athletes world wide and the ultimate showcase for endurance sports.

Colour-photo illustration throughout
200 pages, Hardcover, 10" x 10"
ISBN 1-84126-100-9
£ 19.95 UK / $ 29.95 US
$ 47.95 CDN / € 29.90

Start your Ironman Library today!

- The first ever book about the world's most important endurance sports event – The Ironman Triathlon World Championship

- 200 page, hard cover collection of the greatest moments from the Toughest Day in Sport

- The greatest collection of photos ever assembled

From 1978 to 2002, the Ironman Triathlon World Championship grew from 15 crazies to a world wide extravaganza. This is the first book to capture it all. It's all here. From the first ever Ironman in 1978 to Julie Moss famous crawl to the finish to Mark Allen and Dave Scott's legendary IRONWAR battle on the Queen K Highway.

The great photography and Bob Babbitt's year-by-year commentary make this book a must buy. It captures the drama that is the Ironman.

Find this fantastic book at fine bookstores everywhere!

MEYER & MEYER SPORT

MEYER & MEYER Sport | sales@m-m-sports.com | m-m-sports.com